MW00492259

THE FACTS ON
THE BIBLE

JOHN ANKERBERG
JOHN WELDON &
DILLON BURROUGHS

HARVEST HOUSE PUBLISHERS

EUGENE, OREGON

Cover by Dugan Design Group, Bloomington, Minnesota

Cover photos © Fotolia

Back-cover author photo of Dillon Burroughs © Goldberg Photography

THE FACTS ON THE BIBLE
The Facts On Series
Formerly *The Facts on Why You Can Believe the Bible*, which was adapted with new research from *Knowing the Truth About the Reliability of the Bible*, *The Facts on False Views of Jesus*, and short excerpts from *Ready with an Answer*.
Copyright © 2004 by John Ankerberg and John Weldon
Published by Harvest House Publishers
Eugene, Oregon 97402
www.harvesthousepublishers.com

Library of Congress Cataloging-in-Publication Data
    Ankerberg, John, 1945-
    The facts on the Bible / John Ankerberg and John Weldon.—Updates / by Dillon Burroughs.
        p. cm.—(The facts on series)
    Rev. ed. of: The facts on why you can believe the Bible. © 2004.
    Includes bibliographical references.
    ISBN 978-0-7369-2490-0 (pbk.)
    1. Bible—Evidences, authority, etc. I. Weldon, John II. Ankerberg, John, 1945- Facts on why you can believe the Bible. III. Title.
    BS480.A68 2008
    220.1—dc22
                                                                                    2008032119

Printed in the United States of America

    09 10 11 12 13 14 15 16 17 / VP-NI / 10 9 8 7 6 5 4 3 2 1

Contents

Section Three
The Responsibility of Historical Research

Section Four
Conclusion

The Bible and the Difference It Makes

"So many of the ideas that found application in America's founding documents and our government were taken from the Bible. It is not only the single most cited authority in the writings of the founding era, but it is also the book from which many of America's political and social customs were originally formed."

—David Barton
The Influence of the Bible on America

1

Does the Bible matter?

Christian faith is increasingly under assault today, even in America, a nation that has benefited extraordinarily from its positive influence in national and individual life. Many are now expressing open disdain for the Christian faith that has provided their freedoms. Such disdain could be seen as one of the great ironies of recent time. Those who wish to tear down the Bible and Christian faith should actually be on their knees thanking God for both, because otherwise they would clearly not have the blessings and freedoms for their personal endeavors.

Whatever shortcomings Christian faith has displayed throughout history, they pale into insignificance compared to the incalculable blessings it has produced for America and throughout the world. The benefits are due largely to one factor—the teachings of the Bible lived out in practical ways by men and women who believed it. When we examine the benefits of Christian faith to humankind, we must remember it is the Bible that plays the central role.

Because this book talks about the trustworthiness of the Bible, an appropriate place to begin is by briefly illustrating for readers how the Bible has dramatically impacted their lives.* Put simply, without the influence of the Bible, the United States would not exist, nor would a Western civilization where people have the freedom to censure expressions of Christian faith. Christianity deserves credit for many of the great political, social, humanitarian, scientific, educational, and cultural advances in the Western world. The Bible, it seems, has inspired most of the great writers, artists, educators, scientists, politicians, and educators.

Those who seek to undermine or destroy Christian influence merely engage in a form of cultural suicide: They destroy the very possibility of building the better life they seek.

Examples of areas where Christianity has exerted a profound and positive influence on Western civilization include

- the founding and development of modern science and law

- the founding and development of medicine and health care, involving the first establishing of hospitals

- modern education, including the founding of nearly all major American universities, such as Princeton, Harvard, Yale, and Dartmouth

- providing a logical basis through absolute values for the advance of ethics in general, including

---

* A number of books and papers have been written on this topic, but those we would recommend most for additional study are by Alvin J. Schmidt, *Under the Influence: How Christianity Transformed Civilization;* D. James Kennedy and Jerry Newcombe, *What If Jesus Had Never Been Born?* and *What If the Bible Had Never Been Written?;* and the paper by Professor Paul Johnson, "The Necessity of Christianity."[1]

sexual morality, which in our time alone has saved millions of lives

- protecting the dignity of marriage and family life, which greatly contributes to the stabilization of society

- instituting political freedom and human rights generally, including the abolition of slavery and the protection of the unborn, infants, children, and women

- inspiring major contributions to the best in art, literature, music, and architecture

- undergirding vast humanitarian endeavors globally and supporting the dignity of labor and economic reform

And many more areas of positive influence could be named.

Women, children, slaves, the sick, the unborn, the uneducated, the persecuted, those mentally challenged, abandoned, or dying—almost no category of the vulnerable has been left unembraced by Christian faith. The Red Cross, the Salvation Army, public education (which originated with the Protestant reformers), modern capitalism, property rights and private property, workers' protection, women's rights, political freedom and democracy, the idea of liberty and justice for all— all these owe their support or existence to biblical ideals. The difference between the pre-Christian world and the post-Christian is like night and day, and the Bible made the difference.

One man who believed in the Bible

To cite one example in our modern era, the world itself is safer at present and a nation of some 300 million people is free today because of one man's Christian faith—his personal trust in Christ and his belief in the Bible. President Ronald Reagan played an immense role in bringing down the Soviet Union because he believed he was called to this task and trusted God for the outcome. He won the Cold War and freed the Soviet Union, reinvigorated America, and achieved so much else because he had believed in Christ from a young age, spent hours on his knees in prayer, and was dominated by his faith—undoubtedly one reason his life was so richly blessed.

The near-insurmountable goal of dismantling the godless Soviet state was born in part because of his desire to give the Russian people freedom of religion for their souls' sake. As he explained it in a famous speech on March 8, 1983, that condemned the "Evil Empire," he believed "we're enjoined by Scripture and the Lord Jesus to oppose it with all our might."[2]

All this and more is why those who are Christians should be thankful for the Bible. Those who wish to undermine Christian influence in the world should recognize the recent corrosion of education, law, morality, cultural entertainment (such as TV and music), family life, and even freedom itself. What was once noble and great is increasingly frayed and profane. The more people tear down the Bible and Christian faith, the more they contribute to the very process that will destroy their own and others' future.

Of course, what can never be destroyed is the eternal. The practical day-to-day benefits everyone experiences from the Bible pale in comparison to the spiritual benefits Christian faith has conveyed upon untold millions globally, but that is the subject of another book. Here we discuss *the* Book. In the history of humanity, if even a billion books have been written, only one is extraordinary. Among even the sacred books of the world, none comes close, and one only need read them to appreciate the truth of it. The Bible's influence in history is incalculable: It has literally changed the world—not just Western history, but all of history.*

Given the Bible's impact, it's astonishing that hundreds of millions of people in the most educated nations are fundamentally ignorant of its contents. Since the ideals of education cannot explain it, perhaps only willful unbelief can. As Aldous Huxley once noted, "Most ignorance is vincible ignorance. We don't know because we don't want to know."[3]

Some people prefer not to study the Bible because they intuitively recognize it would interfere with how they wish to live. As a result, the Bible experiences regular assaults on its credibility from biased academics, professional skeptics, religious and cultural leaders, and so on, which are eventually absorbed by the public at large.

In a world of unbelief, only a relatively small percentage of people accept the Bible as the literal, inerrant Word of God. Unfortunately, in addition to philosophical, cultural, and emotional bias, another part of the problem can be found in the Christian church itself. It has often failed to adequately educate its members about the Bible, not only doctrinally but evidentially as well. It is unlikely that a person will grant support to the content of the Bible unless he or she is convinced its content is accurate and authoritative.

Because so many people remain uninformed about the trustworthiness of the Bible, we have written this

---

* A number of quotations from famous historical figures that confirm the Bible's influence are given in "Learning from History" at the end of this book.

book. The simple fact is, two millennia of careful investigation by believers and unbelievers alike have reasonably proven the following assertion: The Bible is the Word of God without demonstrable error—despite its age, its varied authorship, and its many critics.

In this book we will explain why this is so, and also why the Bible's critics lack support. We think it is significant that, given 2,000 years of the most intense scrutiny by critics and skeptics, tens of millions of people in the modern era continue to believe the Bible is the literal, inerrant Word of God—and argue that it can be rationally defended as such. Can members of any other religious faith prove such a claim concerning their own scripture?

2

What have been the different approaches to establishing the reliability of the Bible?

Over time, a variety of well-reasoned and objective approaches for establishing the reliability of the Bible have been employed. Among them are

- *Its prophetic accuracy*—The Bible's remarkable predictions, due to their specific nature, cannot logically be explained apart from divine inspiration and foreknowledge.

- *The testimony of Jesus Christ*—His complete endorsement of the Old Testament as the inerrant Word of God and his pre-authentication of the New Testament offer the strongest proof of biblical trustworthiness, because of who Christ is. Because

Jesus is God incarnate, as proven by his unparalleled life and teachings, spectacular miracles, and resurrection from the dead, he stands as an infallible authority, and in that position he taught that the Bible was the literal Word of God.

- *The manuscript evidence*—This proves the Bible has not experienced textual corruption, as critics argue, but is virtually autographic. (*Autographic* means "original manuscript.")

- *The archaeological data*—The striking fact is, over a century of detailed scientific archaeological excavations have failed to prove a *single* biblical statement incorrect, while confirming as accurate thousands of historical, geographical, and other details in the Bible. This cannot easily be explained apart from divine inspiration, again making the Bible unique among all ancient books ever written.

- *Its scientific prevision*—Scores of biblical statements conform to facts of modern science even before these facts were known, something inexplicable on naturalistic grounds. As with the Bible's prophetic and archaeological accuracy, this can only be explained through divine inspiration.

Beyond all the above, the Bible's unique claims, internal unity, recorded miracles, and historic preservation set it apart from all other books and require an explanation for its origin beyond the natural. Indeed, the Bible's overall uniqueness, dramatic power to change lives, and the simple fact it can still rationally be claimed to be the Word of God and logically defended as such reveal what an amazing book it is.

3

Why is the reliability of the Bible a critical subject for everyone?

The reliability of the Bible is crucial because of its implications. It is the most important book in the world because it alone *is* God's Word. To be ignorant concerning its claims and contents constitutes an abdication of personal responsibility (not to mention public education).

If the Bible *is* the Word of God, then its importance to every person and every culture is obvious. Religious scripture that is simply a human product, false or mythic, can hardly command authority. The question is whether or not there is real evidence to support the Bible's claims to be genuine divine revelation.

If the Bible is the inerrant Word of God and authoritatively answers the fundamental questions of life, who can justify being passive and ignoring its teachings? If the Bible accurately tells us who God is, who we are, why we are here, and what happens when we die, should anyone fail to be impressed? If the Bible gives us reassuring absolutes in a world of soul-destroying relatives, doesn't this introduce profound implications? Who wants to live a life of insecurity and hopelessness when he or she can actually know the truth with certainty?

If people live only for themselves and do whatever they want—often in disregard of others' welfare—isn't the major reason for this because they feel life is meaningless and nothing finally matters but their own interests? If there is no final authority in anything, why not live any way you want? It would be difficult to deny that if people today lived according to most of the Ten Commandments, just a "small" set of laws, many national social issues would be solved or greatly diminished in impact. But people don't live that way because they do not really believe those words and commandments came from God. And they certainly don't believe that God will hold them accountable in the next life for the kind of life they have lived here.

In a word, helping people to trust the Bible and live by its precepts is the single most important contribution that can be made to mankind's direction and future. It is the one single item that, if widely adopted, would solve most of our problems immediately, heal nations and peoples, and help us in every way. If so, then the subject of this book must be of great importance.

To know the Bible is reliable is to know that *all* of what it teaches is reliable. And what it teaches is that the one true God sent his only Son to die for our sins so we could inherit eternal life as a free gift. Such a declaration is unparalleled. If skeptics are given only one reason to examine the claims of the Bible, this should be the paramount one. If true, it offers more than they could possibly imagine. Conversely, if the Bible is trustworthy and one rejects its message of salvation, then no other personal decision will be more consequential. No one can logically fail to ignore the issue of the reliability of the Bible.

4

What does the Bible claim for itself, and is there good reason to believe it?

The Bible contains some 1,200 promises, 3,000 questions, 6,000 commands, and some 8,000 verses having predictions of the future. It mentions God some 10,000 times. And in various ways, the Bible consistently claims to be God's Word—absolutely authoritative, inerrant, immutable, truthful, and eternal:

- "All Scripture is inspired by God" (2 Timothy 3:16 NASB).

- "The Scripture cannot be broken" (John 10:35).

- "Your word is truth" (John 17:17).

- "Heaven and earth will pass away, but my words will never pass away" (Matthew 24:35).

- "Every word of God is tested" (Proverbs 30:5 NASB).

- "The words of the LORD are pure words, as silver tried in a furnace on the earth, refined seven times" (Psalm 12:6 NASB).

- "You have been born again not of seed which is perishable but imperishable, that is, through the living and enduring word of God" (1 Peter 1:23 NASB).

- "Forever, O LORD, your word is settled in heaven" (Psalm 119:89 NASB).

- "Truly I say to you, until heaven and earth pass away, not the smallest letter or stroke shall pass from the Law until all is accomplished" (Matthew 5:18 NASB).

- "[Jesus] answered and said, 'It is written, "Man shall not live on bread alone, but on every word that proceeds out of the mouth of God"'" (Matthew 4:4 NASB).

- "The word of the Lord endures forever" (1 Peter 1:25 NASB).

If the Bible is really the Word of God, an errorless original text is what we would expect from a truthful God.[4] But what a seemingly difficult proposition to defend in a modern scientific world, especially since we don't have the original manuscripts.

Inerrancy defined

A good general definition of biblical inerrancy is given by Dr. Paul Feinberg:

> Inerrancy means that when all facts are known, the Scriptures in their original autographs and properly interpreted will be shown to be wholly true in everything that they affirm, whether that has to do with doctrine or morality or with the social, physical, or life sciences.[5]

Even if we had those manuscripts, could 40-plus writers of highly divergent background and temperament—kings, tax collectors, prophets, physicians, exiles, fishermen—writing over a period of approximately 1,500 years (from 1450 BC to AD 75), on scores of different subjects, in widely varying and difficult circumstances, including persecution; writing history in extremely specific detail, even giving hundreds and hundreds of predictions of the future—plus much more that would make errors a certainty—could all of them to the last man have written something the size of the Bible without a single error? At ten hours a day it takes seven days just to read the Bible—if you read very fast. Talk about the supernatural. Try generating an errorless text that size with 66 books and 40 authors over 1,500 years with any other group of writers in history.

Indeed, just try it with any ten books and five writers over 50 years. Yet the evidence strongly suggests the Bible is inerrant—and again, only divine inspiration can account for it.

There are three principal lines of evidence for the inerrancy of the Bible, properly understood.[6] These involve claim, testimony, and data:

- The Bible's own claim to be the literal word of God, as illustrated above, is not made from thin air, but is supported by its demonstrated credibility in other areas;

- The testimony of Jesus, the final authority in whatever he taught, encompasses the most important evidence; and

- The lack of a single proven error, despite innumerable critical examinations of biblical data.

5

Did Jesus believe the Bible was without error?

For Jesus, what Scripture said, God said—period. Not once did he say, "This Scripture is in error" and proceed to correct it. The testimony of Jesus Christ to the reliability of the Old Testament is indisputable (see John 17:17).

As God (John 1:1; 5:17-18; 10:30), Jesus Christ is omniscient; in that authoritative role he authenticated the strict, literal, historical accuracy of the Old Testament, including the narratives most often rejected as mythological by the critics, such as creation, a world-wide flood, Jonah swallowed by a great fish, Daniel, and so on.

The strength of the case for Jesus' view of inerrancy is seen by a careful study of his absolute trust in and use of Scripture.* If it were otherwise, Jesus would positively have told us that there were errors and corrected them. (But even this is illogical, for it presumes either errant divine inspiration or a lack of providential preservation of the text.) Bible scholar John Murray summarizes Jesus' teaching:

> It is of the Old Testament without any reservation or exception that he says, it "cannot be broken"... He affirms the unbreakableness of the Scripture in its entirety and leaves no room for any such supposition as that of degrees of inspiration and fallibility. Scripture is inviolable. Nothing less than this is the testimony of our Lord. And the crucial nature of such witness is driven home by the fact that it is in answer to the most serious of charges and in the defense of his most stupendous claim that he bears this testimony.[7]

Taking the previous discussion as a basis, consider this line of reasoning about inerrancy,[8] which centers on Christ's resurrection. The following points show definitively that the historical fact of the resurrection proves the inerrancy of the Bible:[9]

1. On the basis of accepted principles of historic and textual analysis, the New Testament documents are shown to be reliable and trustworthy historical documents (see questions 3 and 6).

---

* As seen, for example, in the detailed, authoritative study of Christ's view of Scripture by John Wenham in *Christ and the Bible*.[10]

2. In the Gospel records, Jesus claimed to be God incarnate (John 5:18; 10:27-33). But he didn't just claim this; he proved it like no other person in history. He exercised innumerable divine prerogatives, and he rested his claims on numerous eyewitnesses and historically unparalleled miracles (John 10:37-38), including his physical resurrection from the dead, which he repeatedly prophesied (John 10:17-18).

3. In each Gospel, Christ's resurrection is minutely described, and for 2,000 years it has been undisprovable despite the detailed investigation of the world's best skeptics.

4. In sum, the historic fact of Christ's resurrection from the dead proves his claim to deity.

5. Because Jesus is literally God, he is of necessity an infallible authority, incapable of speaking error (John 12:48-50; Matthew 24:35). And he clearly taught that Scripture originates from God and is inerrant, since that which originates from an utterly trustworthy, immutable God must be utterly trustworthy and immutable itself.

6. Again, if Jesus is God, what God says is true by definition, and therefore Jesus' teaching on the unqualified inerrancy of the Scriptures proves the validity of the inerrancy position.*

If you had to choose, would you choose based on the assertions of scholars who begin from groundless critical

---

* In John 17:17 and Matthew 4:4, Jesus could have referred only to the complete Old Testament canon of the Jews then extant (Luke 24:27). He affirmed 100 percent of the Old Testament as inspired and therefore inerrant. (See John 1:1; 5:46; 8:14-16,26,28; 12:48-50; 14:6; 2 Peter 1:20; Philippians 2:1-8; Titus 2:13.)

assumptions—people who have never performed even one miracle—or on the assertions of the only man in history to claim beforehand that he would rise from the dead...and actually do it? As theologian, historian, and trial attorney, Dr. John Warwick Montgomery observes,

> The weight of Christ's testimony to Scripture is so much more powerful than any alleged contradiction or error in the text or any combination of them, that the latter must be adjusted to the former, not the reverse.[11]

Finally, evidence for inerrancy is seen in the biblical data itself: 1) Despite some problems that are still irresolvable because of insufficient information, no error has ever been proven (again, a virtual miracle). And 2) it is simply impossible to account for books like Zephaniah, Obadiah, and Nahum, which are over 70 percent predictive and all of whose past predictions have come about—apart from the existence of an omniscient God who knows the future and has reliably revealed it.

The Accuracy and Supernatural Character of the Biblical Text

6

Why would anyone argue that the Bible can't be trusted?

Otherwise brilliant scientists, skeptics, college students, and university professors argue that the Bible cannot be trusted. However attentive they may be to facts in other areas, in this area they speak largely on the basis of unjustified assumptions, bias, or simple ignorance of the facts. How do we know that the Bible is accurate and trustworthy in history, religion, science, and whatever else it may speak on? Consider seven points that the factually challenged normally ignore.

Fact one: Manuscript preservation

The biblical text is far more accurately preserved than any other text of ancient history. There are far more New Testament manuscripts copied with far greater accuracy and dating far earlier than is the case for any secular classic from antiquity. For the New Testament, we have a fragment written within about a generation of its original composition; whole books written within about 100 years from the time of the originals; most of the New Testament in less than 200 years, and the entire New Testament within 250 years, from the date of its completion. Collectively, there are thousands of New Testament manuscripts and portions.[1]

The Gospels' composition was extremely close chronologically to the events they record. The writing of the first three can be dated as early as within 20 years or so of the events cited, and this may even be true for the fourth Gospel (see fact six). Regardless, all four Gospels were written during the lives of eyewitnesses to the events they recorded, and abundant opportunity existed for those with contrary evidence to examine the witnesses and refute them.

The Old Testament was also incredibly preserved, and its overall historical accuracy has been factually confirmed.*

For example, a detailed comparison of the Qumran Old Testament manuscripts (dating back to the 200s BC) and the Masoretic Old Testament texts (from the AD 900s) reveals, in the words of Dr. Ron Rhodes, that "they are essentially the same, with very few changes," despite more than 1,000 years of copying.[2] The fact that manuscripts separated by a thousand years are essentially the same indicates the incredible accuracy of the Old Testament's manuscript transmission. Indeed, if the Bible were simply an assortment of secular writings, no fair-minded scholar in the world would suggest that its text was unreliable. While collectively there are thousands of copies of the individual biblical books, and while these manuscript copies differ, as one would expect, the differences are typically minor, and none have major impact.

Textual reconstruction

Dr. Ron Rhodes supplies the following New Testament illustration:

Manuscript 1: **Jesus** Christ is the Redeemer of the whole **worl**.

Manuscript 2: **Christ** Jesus is the Redeemer of the whole world.

---

* As illustrated in scholarly texts such as K.A. Kitchen's *On the Reliability of the Old Testament* (2003) and Walter Kaiser's *The Old Testament Documents: Are They Reliable and Relevant?* (2001).

Manuscript 3: Jesus Christ s the Redeemer of the whole world.

Manuscript 4: Jesus Christ is **th** Redeemer of the **whle** world.

Manuscript 5: Jesus Christ is the Redeemer of the whole **wrld**.[3]

Reconstructing the original from these five sample "manuscripts" is easy, as it is for the entire New Testament in general—to an accuracy of more than 99 percent, with the remaining uncertainties being insignificant.

There are 5,300 extant Greek manuscripts and portions, 10,000 of the Latin Vulgate, and 9,300 of other versions. As previously noted, the papyri and early uncial manuscripts date much closer to the originals than is the case with any other ancient literature. For example, considering 16 well-known classical authors (Plutarch, Tacitus, Suetonius, Polybius, Thucydides, Xenophon, and others), the total number of extant copies of their manuscripts is typically less than *ten*, and the earliest copies date from 750 to 1,600 years *after* the original manuscript was first penned.[4] We need only compare this slender evidence to the mass of biblical documentation involving over 24,000 manuscript portions, manuscripts, and versions, the earliest fragments and complete copies dating between 50 and 300 years after the originals were written.

No ancient literature has ever supplied historians and textual critics with such an abundance of data. It is this wealth of material that has enabled scholars such as Westcott and Hort, Ezra Abbott, Philip Schaff, A.T. Robertson, Norman Geisler, and William Nix to place the restoration of the original text at 99-percent-plus accuracy.[5] For example, Hort's estimate of "substantial variation" for the New Testament is one-tenth of

1 percent, and Abbot's estimate is one-fourth of 1 percent. (Hort's figure including "trivial variations" is still
less than 2 percent.) Sir Frederic Kenyon well summarizes the situation:

> The number of manuscripts of the New Testament…is
> so large that it is practically certain that the true reading
> of every doubtful passage is preserved in some one or
> another of these ancient authorities. This can be said
> of no other ancient book in the world.[6]

How can the New Testament possibly be rejected as
textually "unreliable" when its documentation is at least
100 times that of other ancient literature—literature
that is widely accepted as reliable? In other words, those
who question the reliability of the Bible must also question the reliability of virtually every ancient writing the
world possesses! In effect, to throw out the Bible is to
throw out ancient history altogether.

Fact two: Archaeology

Archaeology has repeatedly and dramatically confirmed the accuracy of the biblical narratives in both
Testaments. What scholars once considered myths are,
time and again, proven facts of history. (See question 7
for further discussion.)

Fact three: Incontrovertible conviction of truth

No proven fraud or error exists on the part of any of
the 40 New or Old Testament authors. Do the writers
contradict themselves? Is there anything in their writing
which causes a reader to objectively suspect their trustworthiness? The answer is no. But there is evidence of
careful eyewitness reporting throughout the New and
Old Testaments. The caution exercised by the writers,

their personal conviction that what they wrote was true, and the lack of demonstrable error or contradiction indicate that the authors told the truth.*

As far as the New Testament, for example, the apostle John emphasized, speaking of himself, "This is the disciple who testifies to these things [about Jesus] and who wrote them down. We know that his testimony is true" (John 21:24). The physician Luke emphasized his personal care in reporting: "I myself have carefully investigated everything from the beginning...so that you may know the certainty of the things you have been taught" (Luke 1:3-4). "After his [Jesus'] suffering, he showed himself to these men [apostles] and gave many convincing proofs that he was alive. He appeared to them over a period of forty days and spoke about the kingdom of God" (Acts 1:3).

Luke's careful historical writing was documented from detailed archaeological data by former skeptic Sir William Ramsay, who stated after his painstaking investigations, "Luke's history is unsurpassed in respect of its trustworthiness." A.N. Sherwin-White, the distinguished historian of Rome, stated of Luke: "For [the book of] Acts the confirmation of historicity is overwhelming. Any attempt to reject its basic historicity even in matters of detail must now appear absurd."[7]

The many powerful enemies of Jesus and the early church would have proven fraud or pointed out other serious problems had they been able to—but their silence is deafening. Their complete inability to discredit Christian claims (when they had both the motive and ability to do so) argues strongly for the veracity of the Gospel authors.

---

* See Luke 1:1-4; John 19:35; 21:24; Acts 1:1-3; 2:22; 26:24-26; 2 Peter 1:16; 1 John 1:1-3.

Fact four: Sources outside the New Testament

The Church Fathers extensively cite the New Testament. There are some 36,000 early (AD 100–300) patristic quotations of the New Testament—such that all but a few verses of the entire New Testament could be reconstructed from these alone.[8]

In addition, the existence of both Jewish and secular accounts confirm to a significant degree the picture of Christ we have in the New Testament. For example, research by Dr. Gary R. Habermas in his book *Ancient Evidence for the Life of Jesus* and other works indicates that "a broad outline of the life of Jesus" and his death by crucifixion can be reasonably and directly inferred from entirely non-Christian sources.[9]

Fact five: Eyewitnesses

The presence of hundreds of eyewitnesses to the events recorded in the New Testament would surely have prohibited any major distortion of the facts, just as today any false reporting as to a major event witnessed by hundreds of people would be corrected on the basis of living eyewitnesses and historic records. The Gospel writers could not have gotten away with myth-making, given what was at stake for both Christ's followers and his enemies. They time and again maintained that the events had happened openly, that they were literally eyewitnesses of the miraculous events of Jesus' life, and that their testimony should be believed because it was true:

- "We are witnesses of these things" (Acts 5:32).

- "We did not follow cleverly invented stories" (2 Peter 1:16).

- "I stand here and testify to small and great alike. I am saying nothing beyond what the prophets and Moses said would happen…What I am saying is true and reasonable. The king is familiar with these things, and I can speak freely to him. I am convinced that none of this has escaped his notice, because it was not done in a corner" (Acts 26:22,25-26).

Significantly, unlike any other religious leader, Jesus frequently appealed to his ability to prove his claims to deity by predicting the future or performing spectacular miracles, such as healing those born blind or raising the dead: "I am telling you now before it happens, so that when it does happen you will believe that I am He" (John 13:19). "Believe me when I say that I am in the Father and the Father is in me; or at least believe on the evidence of the miracles themselves" (John 14:11).

When Jesus healed the paralytic (Mark 2:8-11), he did so "that you may know that the Son of Man has authority on earth to forgive sins"—for Jews, an obvious claim to being God. In John 10:33 the Jewish leaders accused Jesus of blaspheming because he was claiming to be God. What was Jesus' response?

> Do not believe me unless I do what my Father does. But if I do it, even though you do not believe me, believe the miracles, that you may know and understand that the Father is in me, and I in the Father (John 10:37-38).

This is another evident claim to deity. Many other examples could be added showing the power of eyewitness testimony to biblical reliability.

Fact six: Critics and skeptics

Both conservative scholars, such as F.F. Bruce and John Wenham, and liberal scholars, such as Bishop A.T. Robinson, have penned defenses of New Testament reliability. This is testimony to the strength of the data. For example, in *Redating Matthew, Mark and Luke*, British scholar John Wenham presents a convincing argument that the synoptic (first three) Gospels are to be dated before AD 55. He dates Matthew at AD 40 (some traditions say the early 30s); Mark at AD 45, and Luke no later than AD 51 to 55.[10] Liberal bishop John A.T. Robinson argues in his *Redating the New Testament* that the entire New Testament was written and in circulation between AD 40 and 65.[11] But it would not surprise us to discover, in the end, that the synoptics were written before AD 40, within ten years of the death of Christ.[12]

The implications of this early dating are immense. A New Testament written before AD 75 destroys the edifice on which higher critical premises regarding the New Testament are based. Insufficient time is available for the early church to have, as has been suggested, embellished the records with their own alleged inventions about Jesus.

Even the critical methods themselves indirectly support New Testament reliability because consistent scholarly, factual reversals of their conclusions undermine *their* credibility, not the Bible's. Although higher critical theories reject biblical reliability by mere supposition, nevertheless, when such theories

> are subjected to the same analytical scrutiny as they apply to the New Testament documents, they will be found to make their own contribution to validating the historicity of those records.[13]

Even 200 years of scholarly rationalistic biblical criticism (such as form, source, and redaction approaches) have proven nothing except that the New Testament writers were careful and honest reporters of the events recorded and that the methods attempting to discredit them are flawed and biased from the start.[14] The fact that critics and skeptics have done so poorly over the ages says more than they are willing to concede.

Convinced by the evidence

Think about the many capable or brilliant skeptics in every generation who have converted to Christianity largely on the basis of the historical evidence—Saul of Tarsus, Athenagoras, Augustine, George Lyttleton and Gilbert West, Cyril Joad, John Warwick Montgomery, C.S. Lewis, Frank Morison, Sir William Ramsay, Malcolm Muggeridge, Lew Wallace, and Lee Strobel. For Bible critics to be right, such men must be either naïve or deceived.[15]

Fact seven: Legal evidence

Many additional logical and legal reasons document biblical reliability. For example, critics argue that Jesus Christ was not who the disciples claim he was in the New Testament, but merely an unusual Jewish prophet whom the disciples made into a divine savior. Now, what this means is that the disciples all suffered severe persecution and later died for what they *knew* was false. If anything is illogical, it's sacrificing your life for what you know is a lie. The disciples gave their lives solely because the evidence convinced them Christ was who he claimed to be; mere subjective "evidence" had nothing to do with it.

Lawyers, of course, are expertly trained in the matter of evaluating evidence and are perhaps the most qualified in the task of weighing data critically. Is it coincidence that so many of the best legal minds throughout history have concluded in favor of the truth of the Christian religion, and on the grounds of strict legal evidence alone have accepted the New Testament as factual history?

Consider the "father of international law," Hugo Grotius, who wrote *The Truth of the Christian Religion* (1627); or the single greatest authority on English and American common-law evidence in the nineteenth century, Harvard Law School professor Simon Greenleaf, who wrote *Testimony of the Evangelists*, in which he powerfully demonstrated the reliability of the Gospels.[16] There is also Edmund H. Bennett (1824–1898), who for over 20 years was the Dean of Boston University Law School and penned *The Four Gospels from a Lawyer's Standpoint* (1899).[17] Attorney Irwin Linton represented cases before the Supreme Court and wrote *A Lawyer Examines the Bible* (1943, 1977), in which he stated,

> So invariable had been my observation that he who does not accept wholeheartedly the evangelical, conservative belief in Christ and the Scriptures has never read, has forgotten, or never been able to weigh—and certainly is utterly unable to refute—the irresistible force of the cumulative evidence upon which such faith rests, that there seems ample ground for the conclusion that such ignorance is an invariable element in such unbelief. And this is so even though the unbeliever be a preacher, who is supposed to know this subject if he know no other.[18]

Such men were certainly acquainted with legal reasoning and have just as certainly concluded that the evidence for the historic truthfulness of Scripture is beyond reasonable doubt. As John Warwick Montgomery observes in *The Law Above the Law*, the following factors all coalesce directly or indirectly to support the preponderance of evidence for Christianity:

- *The "ancient documents" rule*: that ancient documents constitute competent evidence if there is no evidence of tampering and they have been accurately transmitted.

- *The "parol evidence" rule*: that Scripture must interpret itself without foreign intervention.

- *The "hearsay" rule*: that primary-source evidence is demanded.

- *The "cross examination" principle*: that the enemies of Christianity were unable to disprove its central claim that Christ was resurrected bodily from the dead in spite of the motive and opportunity to do so.

Based on the above, concludes Montgomery, the burden of proof proper (the legal burden) for disproving the truthfulness of Scripture rests with the critic—who, in 2,000 years, has yet to make a case.[19]

The above seven facts—textual accuracy; archaeological confirmation; accurate reporting and conviction of truth, especially that of Jesus Christ; extrabiblical corroboration; numerous eyewitness accounts to the events; critics' and skeptics' contributions; and additional logical and legal considerations—demonstrate the reliability of the Bible.

In sum, what this means is that we can trust what the biblical authors say as being true.

7

Does biblical archaeology confirm the reliability of the Bible?

Biblical archaeology does confirm the Bible's trust-worthiness—greatly—primarily by demonstrating that it is dependable whenever archaeological discoveries come to bear on its text. Archaeology cannot be expected to confirm the Bible's every statement about history, geography, culture, and so on, because the amount of information archaeology has uncovered is still relatively small. In addition, there are sometimes problems with interpretation of the data.

However, when sufficient factual information becomes known and is properly interpreted, it confirms the biblical record. In cases where a discovery initially seems not to confirm the Bible, there is never sufficient factual data to disprove a biblical statement. Given the thousands of minute details in the Bible that archaeology has the opportunity to disprove, this confirmation of the biblical record is striking. For example, even 50 years ago "over 25,000 sites from the biblical world" had been "confirmed by some archaeological discoveries to date."[20]

Material confirmation of the Bible leads people to have confidence in the Bible's spiritual teachings. In other words, those who believe that the Bible is unreliable in archaeological and historical matters can hardly be expected to accept its teachings in spiritual matters. To illustrate, a famous author's cookbook may promise heavenly culinary delights, but if the recipe ingredients are wrong, the promise won't matter.

Concerning the Bible's spiritual teachings, when

we add together the words of the Gospel of Luke and the book of Acts, we discover that the physician Luke wrote fully one-fourth of the entire New Testament. We mentioned earlier that his detailed accuracy has been confirmed by modern archaeology. It is this very same careful historian who reports that Jesus Christ was physically resurrected from the dead by "many convincing proofs" (Acts 1:3)—and that he had carefully investigated the evidence for this from the beginning (Luke 1:1-4).

If Luke was so painstakingly accurate in his historical reporting,* on what reasonable basis may we assume he was credulous or inaccurate in his reporting of matters that were far more important—not only to him but to everyone else as well? Luke's meticulous accuracy in historical, geographical, political, and cultural matters lends weight to his claims concerning the resurrection of Christ, even though he is dealing with an unparalleled miraculous event.

Considering the Old Testament, archaeology has proven the biblical record time and again. *The New International Dictionary of Biblical Archaeology*, written by a score of experts in various fields, shows this repeatedly. For instance:

> Near Eastern archaeology has demonstrated the historical and geographical reliability of the Bible in many important areas...It is now known, for instance, that, along with the Hittites, Hebrew scribes were the *best historians in the entire ancient Near East*, despite contrary propaganda that emerged from Assyria, Egypt, and elsewhere.[21]

---

* For example, he names 32 countries, 54 cities, 9 islands, and much else without error.

John Arthur Thompson was also director of the Australian Institute of Archaeology in Melbourne and has done archaeological fieldwork with the American Schools of Oriental Research. In *The Bible and Archaeology* he writes, "If one impression stands out more clearly than any other today, it is that on all hands the overall historicity of the Old Testament tradition is admitted." Norman Geisler and Ron Brooks point out,

> In every period of Old Testament history, we find that there is good evidence from archaeology that the scriptures are accurate…While many have doubted the accuracy of the Bible, time and continued research have consistently demonstrated that the Word of God is better informed than its critics.[22]

Besides what has already been mentioned about the Gospel of Luke, the reliability of the rest of the New Testament is also confirmed by archaeological data. Geisler and Brooks note that "the evidence for its historical reliability [is] overwhelming." John Warwick Montgomery summarizes, "Modern archaeological research has confirmed again and again the reliability of New Testament geography, chronology, and general history." [23]

Three of the greatest American archaeologists of the twentieth century—W.F. Albright, Nelson Glueck, and George Ernest Wright—each had their skeptical liberal training altered by their archaeological work, bolstering their confidence in the biblical text. Albright said of the Bible that "discovery after discovery has established the accuracy of innumerable details."[24] Glueck came to trust what he termed "the remarkable phenomenon of historical memory in the Bible" and forthrightly declared, "It may be clearly stated categorically that no archaeological discovery has ever controverted a single biblical reference."[25] How can we account for such a fact apart from divine inspiration?

Massive vindication

The 17-volume *Archaeology, the Bible and Christ* by Dr. Clifford Wilson, former director of the Australian Institute of Archaeology in Melbourne, brings together more than 5,000 facts relating archaeology to the Bible. Wilson closes volume 17 by pointing out,

> The Bible stands investigation in ways that are unique in all literature. Its superiority to attack, its capacity to withstand criticism, its amazing facility to be proved right after all are all staggering by any standards of scholarship. Seemingly assured results "disproving" the Bible have a habit of backfiring. Over and over again the Bible has been vindicated. That is true from Genesis to Revelation.[26]

Indeed, biblical archaeology continues to offer frustration to Bible critics. Millar Burrows of Yale points out that "archaeology has in many cases refuted the views of modern critics. It has been shown in a number of instances that these views rest on false assumptions and unreal, artificial schemes of historical development," and "the excessive skepticism of many liberal theologians stems not from a careful evaluation of the available data, but from an enormous predisposition against the supernatural."[27] And the noted classical scholar E.M. Blaiklock once wrote,

> Recent archaeology has destroyed much nonsense and will destroy more. And I use the word nonsense deliberately, for theories and speculations find currency in biblical scholarship that would not be tolerated for a moment in any other branch of literary or historical criticism.[28]

The double standard of skeptical critical scholarship is illustrated in its double-minded approach. On the one hand, anytime archaeology does not directly confirm something the Bible teaches, the tendency is to allege an error. On the other hand, critics frequently tend to avoid using archaeology when it confirms the Bible.[29] Indeed, when one considers the archaeological negation of the dominant liberal theories and methods in biblical studies—such as the documentary hypothesis of the Pentateuch, the alleged "Q" source for the New Testament, and form criticism[30]—critics have often ignored archaeology when it discredits theories that they have held to for personal rather than persuasive reasons.

8

What about alleged Bible errors and contradictions?

Far too many people have uncritically accepted the claims of skeptics that the biblical accounts have errors or conflicts and are thus unreliable, and that therefore the Bible itself should not be trusted. The vast majority of alleged contradictions result from two major factors:

1. hasty or casual examination of the text

2. the faulty assumptions and methods of the biased critics—for example, authors' selective use of data.

Careful analysis invariably reveals that no error or contradiction exists. When basic principles for dealing with alleged errors or discrepancies are followed, the great majority of supposed problems are resolved merely by a judicious evaluation of the biblical text itself.[31]

First, the proper definitions of contradiction *and* error *must be observed.* Many who write on these subjects carve out errors themselves because they do not understand or follow the standard dictionary meaning of these terms. In other words, what counts as a contradiction or error? Some set their own rules and create errors based on these guidelines.

Second, rather than presuppose error, impartial critical scholarship would assume the writer is being honest until *proven otherwise,* even when a critic does not like the writer's conclusions. Thus, the limitations on human knowledge should be granted—no critic is omniscient, and none have perfect knowledge. However, every alleged error or contradiction in Scripture has been proven a truthful statement once sufficient historical, archaeological, or other information has been discovered. This gives one full confidence that problems currently irresolvable for lack of data will eventually have a similar outcome.

Third, first impressions can be deceptive. Unless a critic understands what an author has actually said, he or she will be incapable of interpreting him properly. Serious study must be given to all relevant areas: original languages, history, literary form, immediate and larger contexts, geography, culture, sound principles of literary interpretation, archaeological data, specialized use of terms, and so on. (For instance, principles of interpretation that apply to one literary form do not always apply to another.) In fact, the large majority of apparent errors and contradictions result precisely from lack of thorough understanding of the text. For example, the works of Drs. John W. Haley, William Arndt, and Gleason Archer collectively examine over a thousand alleged Bible errors and contradictions, almost all of which are adequately resolved by careful attention to relevant detail.[32]

Fourth, mere differences do not constitute contradictions. Writers have the right to select those facts that fit their purposes and to disregard others, as in the differing Gospel accounts. Critics who will not accept this principle are applying a standard to the biblical writers that they would apply to no one else, themselves included.

Fifth, critics need to try to impartially reexamine their own biases and the validity of their critical theories and methods, whether the documentary hypothesis of Moses' writings, the late date (165 BC) for Daniel, the notion of multiple authors for Isaiah, the assumption of proven contradictions in the differing resurrection accounts, form and redaction criticism, and on and on. Put simply, critics seem to dislike most biblical books because they claim to be revelations from God and contain amazing predictions of the future, something critics rule out as impossible to begin with. Rather than accept even the possibility of divine revelation, skeptics and liberal theologians would prefer to spend vast amounts of time defending artificial speculations.

For ages, critics have proposed their theories—and yet these theories have never marshaled legitimate evidence in their support. They are speculations plucked out of the air for personal and philosophical reasons, not because textual, historical, archaeological, or other data suggest they are true. The actual data are solidly on the side of the Bible, not the critics, as numerous scholarly and popular texts have demonstrated.[33] Indeed, what K.A. Kitchen declares of the dominant critical theory on the books of Moses, termed the *documentary hypothesis*, is true for critical theories generally, despite their widespread acceptance in intellectual circles:

> Even the most ardent advocate of the documentary theory must admit that we have as yet *no single scrap* of external, objective *material* [that is, tangible] evidence for either the existence or the history of "J," "E," or any other alleged source-document.[34]

In sum, the fair use of critical scholarship will support the trustworthiness of the Bible—it's just a shame it is so infrequently employed.

The information discussed to this point should help us take more seriously the Bible's claim to inerrancy, which is something unique among all the ancient books of the world. It is a fact that can be explained only through divine revelation. In a word, God wrote the Bible. That's why we should carefully listen to it.

9

Does the biblical data by itself prove that the Bible is without error?

Modern scientific rationalism has explained very little of the heights and depths of the universe. It is mere speculation to assume that an infinite personal God could never communicate his revelation truthfully and without error.

Inerrancy cannot be 100-percent factually proven only because our knowledge and interpretation are not

100-percent perfect. If they were, based on all the evidence to date, there is every reason to believe inerrancy would be fully demonstrated as such. This is why many leading scholars concur that the problems critics say confront the principle of inerrancy aren't problems at all. Dr. John Warwick Montgomery writes,

> I myself have never encountered an alleged contradiction in the Bible which could not be cleared up by the use of the original languages of the Scriptures and/or by the use of accepted principles of literary and historical interpretation.[35]

Dr. Gleason L. Archer agrees:

> As I have dealt with one apparent discrepancy after another and have studied the alleged contradictions between the biblical record and the evidence of linguistics, archaeology, or science, my confidence in the trustworthiness of Scripture has been repeatedly verified and strengthened by the discovery that almost every problem in Scripture that has ever been discovered by man, from ancient times until now, has been dealt with in a completely satisfactory manner by the biblical text itself—or else by objective archaeological information.[36]

Dr. William Arndt concluded, in his own study of alleged contradictions and errors in the Bible, that "we may say with full conviction that no instances of this sort occur anywhere in the Scriptures."[37]

We stress again, given the phenomena of Scripture in general, that the biblical text should at least be considered innocent until proven guilty. If *people* are presumed innocent until proven guilty, how is it we presume

God—after he supplies sufficient evidence for belief—is still pronounced guilty?

Someone must be the judge of Scripture. Either it must be a perfect God, who has already testified to its authority and inerrancy (Isaiah 40:8; John 5:46-47; 10:35) or it must be imperfect critics, who judge God to be in error. In spite of the evidence, skeptics somehow assume error where Jesus declares truth; somehow assert the superiority of finite and fallible human reason above divine revelation; and somehow assume the legitimacy of theory and myth over fact. Sadly, because they establish an authoritative criterion above that of God himself, they commit a form of idolatry.

10

Does prophecy prove the Bible is God's only revelation to man?

On earth, only one religion's Scriptures have specific predictions of the future. It's fair to conclude that these Scriptures alone comprise a divine revelation. A central purpose of the Bible's prophecy is just this—to reveal the one true God "so that all the peoples of the earth may know that the LORD is God and that there is no other" (1 Kings 8:60; see verses 1-59).

God teaches that his knowledge of the future is proof that he alone is the Lord. No one else has consistently told of things to come and also had them come true exactly as forecast (see Isaiah 41:20-29). God did this "so that people may see and know, may consider and understand, that the hand of the LORD has done this" (Isaiah 41:20). God challenges men to put him to the test, so that even the skeptics and stubborn-hearted will have no excuse for rejecting him (Isaiah 48:3-7).

The reason we know biblical prophecies are genuine is because they are given by God himself. "All Scripture is inspired by God" (2 Timothy 3:16 NASB); "Prophecy never had its origin in the will of man, but men spoke from God as they were carried along by the Holy Spirit" (2 Peter 1:21). In fact, God promises 100-percent reliability in his predictions of the future. One of his prophets is "recognized as one truly sent by the LORD only if his prediction comes true" (Jeremiah 28:9; see Deuteronomy 18:21-22).

Accurate prediction of the future is the domain of the Bible exclusively—and one of the great proofs that it alone is of divine origin. Approximately 27 percent of the entire Bible contains prophetic material—an astonishing figure for so large a book. Prophecies are found in 62 of the 66 books of the Bible. According to a standard encyclopedia on the subject,

> Of the OT's 23,210 verses, 6,641 contain predictive material, or 28½ percent. Out of the NT's 7,914 verses, 1,711 contain predictive material, or 21½ percent. So for the entire Bible's 31,124 verses, 8,352 contain predictive material, or 27 percent of the whole.[38]

Assured fulfillment

Of the 8,352 verses in the Bible that contain predictive material—about 22 percent—more than 1,800 verses, including 318 in the New Testament—deal with the *Second* Coming of Christ.[39] If this means anything, it means that the prediction of the physical return of Jesus Christ to the earth has the same chance of being fulfilled as all of the other prophecies—100 percent.[40]

Examples of fulfilled prophecy to consider

King Josiah. In a prophecy to King Jeroboam (930–909 BC), King Josiah was predicted by name and lineage some *300 years* before he ruled from Jerusalem: "This is what the LORD says: 'A son named Josiah will be born to the house of David'" (1 Kings 13:2). Josiah was a contemporary of Pharaoh Neco, King of Egypt (610–595 BC; 2 Kings 23:29). God also predicted that this king would destroy the altar at Bethel after sacrificing its evil prophets and burning their bones upon it. All this happened exactly as was prophesied 300 years earlier (see 2 Kings 23:14-19).

Bethlehem. The prophet Micah, some 700 years in advance, predicted by name the very town and region of the birthplace of the Messiah, Jesus. He was also predicted to be eternal and the ruler of Israel:

> As for you, Bethlehem Ephrathah [Ephrathah is the region in which Bethlehem was located]...from you One will go forth for Me to be ruler in Israel. His goings forth are from long ago, from the days of eternity (Micah 5:2 NASB).

The Babylonian captivity. The internal and external evidence in the book of Isaiah shows it was written approximately during the years 720–680 BC.[41] The book of Isaiah was definitely in existence 100 years before the Babylonians conquered Judah. Yet in Isaiah 39:5-7, we find the Babylonian captivity of 586 BC predicted:

> Isaiah said to Hezekiah, "Hear the word of the LORD Almighty: The time will surely come when everything in your palace, and all that your fathers have stored up until this day, will be carried off to Babylon. Nothing will

be left, says the LORD. And some of your descendants, your own flesh and blood who will be born to you, will be taken away, and they will become eunuchs in the palace of the King of Babylon" (see Daniel 1:1-3).

Future kingdoms. The internal and external evidence demand an approximately 530 BC composition for the book of Daniel. Yet the prophet Daniel (Matthew 24:15) predicts the Medo-Persian, Greek, and Roman Empires (chapters 2, 7, 8) in such detail that anti-supernaturalists are forced, against all the evidence, to date the book at 165 BC, implying that it is essentially a forgery.[42]

King Cyrus. Isaiah predicted a very important Persian king by name some 100 years before he was born. The prophet predicted King Cyrus (ruled 559–530 BC) as the one who would permit the Jews to return to their land after the Babylonian captivity, a return that began in 538 BC (Isaiah 44:24–45:6). Once again, the reason God does this is so man will understand and know that he alone is the one true God:

> This is what the LORD says to his anointed, to Cyrus, whose right hand I take hold of to subdue nations before him...so that you may know that I am the LORD, the God of Israel, who summons you by name...I am the LORD, and there is no other; apart from me there is no God (Isaiah 45:1,3,5).

Ezra records the fulfillment of this prophecy in chapter 1 of his book, referring to related prophecies in Jeremiah (Ezra 1:1-11; Jeremiah 25:11-12; 29:10-14).

Messianic prophecy. Finally, consider a small sampling

of Jesus' exact fulfillment of Old Testament Messianic prophecies. How can these be accounted for apart from divine foreknowledge?

1. He would be born of a virgin (Isaiah 7:14; Matthew 1:23).

2. He would live in Nazareth of Galilee (Isaiah 9:1-2; Matthew 2:22-23; 4:15).

3. He would occasion the massacre of Bethlehem's children (Jeremiah 31:15; Matthew 2:16-18).

4. His mission would include the Gentiles (Isaiah 42:1-3,6; Matthew 12:18-21), and he would be rejected by most of the Jews, his own people (Psalm 118:22; 1 Peter 2:7).

5. His ministry would include miracles (Isaiah 35:1-6; 61:1-2; Matthew 9:35; Luke 4:16-21); he would be the Shepherd struck with the sword, resulting in the sheep being scattered (Zechariah 13:7; Matthew 26:31,56; Mark 14:27,49-50).

6. He would be betrayed by a friend for 30 pieces of silver (Zechariah 11:12-13; Matthew 27:7-10).

7. He would die a humiliating death (Psalm 22; Isaiah 53), including rejection (Isaiah 53:3; John 1:10-11; 7:5,48); silence before his accusers (Isaiah 53:7; Matthew 27:12-14); being mocked (Psalm 22:7; Matthew 27:31); the piercing of his hands and feet (Psalm 22:16; Luke 23:33); being crucified with thieves (Isaiah 53:12; Matthew 27:38) yet praying for his persecutors (Isaiah 53:12; Luke 23:43); having lots cast for his garments (Psalm 22:18; John 19:23-24); the piercing of his side

(Zechariah 12:10; John 19:34); being given vinegar and gall to drink (Psalm 69:21; Matthew 27:34); and being buried in a rich man's tomb (Isaiah 53:9; Matthew 27:57-60). He would also rise from the dead (Psalm 16:10; Mark 16:6; Acts 2:31); ascend into heaven (Psalm 68:18; Acts 1:9), and sit down at God's right hand (Psalm 110:1; Hebrews 1:3).[43]

Some 1,800 prophecies in the Bible are best explained by divine foreknowledge and sovereignty and by no other reason. Even skeptics will admit that specific predicting of the future is a miracle, so perhaps they should reconsider their premises.[44]

11

What can skeptics learn from science and mathematics about the Bible?

Over the years we have had various skeptics and critics of the Bible as guests on *The John Ankerberg Show*. Neither from the guests on our TV show or our reading of the skeptical literature have we ever found a legitimate argument against the Bible that would stand the weight of scrutiny. Taken as a whole, skeptics don't believe the Bible simply because they don't want to believe it.

How do we know this? Because, historically, thousands of former skeptics have become Christians on the *basis of the evidence*. If that evidence didn't exist or weren't persuasive, these former skeptics would never have become Christians. Though no amount of evidence will convince someone against his or her will, for the open-minded the evidence is more than sufficient to establish belief.

Two areas in particular that may interest open-minded skeptics are the *scientific prevision* found in the Bible and the *mathematical factors* in favor of its divine inspiration as seen through prophecy.

The unique scientific prevision of the Bible

In the book *The Creator Beyond Time and Space*, Mark Eastman, MD, and Chuck Missler, a computer specialist, provide many examples showing how the Bible, scientifically speaking, was thousands of years ahead of its time. They point out that "there are dozens of passages in the Bible which demonstrate tremendous scientific foreknowledge." Further,

> when the biblical text is carefully examined the reader will quickly discover an uncanny scientific accuracy unparalleled by any document of antiquity...In virtually all ancient religious documents it is common to find scientifically inaccurate myths about the nature of the universe and the life forms on planet earth...However... throughout the Bible we find scientifically accurate concepts about the physical universe that were not "discovered" by modern scientists until very recent times.[45]

For skeptics to successfully maintain that the Bible is not the inspired Word of God, they must explain how the Bible contains accurate scientific information that was often disharmonious with the accepted knowledge of the time. "To argue that the evidence for biblical inspiration is the result of a myriad of lucky guesses requires an enormous measure of faith"[46]—because we know that it is impossible for people to write science and history in advance apart from divine inspiration.

Another prime example is *The Biblical Basis for Modern Science*, in which Dr. Henry Morris, author of some two dozen books on the Bible and science, offers a large number of additional examples of scientific foreknowledge or allusions in the Bible. In the above two books, examples are provided from physics, astronomy, oceanography, the earth's hydrologic cycle, meteorology, medicine, geology, and biology.

In sum, many leading scientists have been very impressed by the scientific accuracy of the Bible. One of them was the late A.E. Wilder-Smith, who held three earned doctorates in science.*

In *The Reliability of the Bible*, Wilder-Smith discussed the historic and prophetic accuracy of Scripture. He commented upon those with initial doubts about the scientific accuracy of the Bible, "Many leading scientists and philosophers, past and present, accepted the entire Bible because they actually researched these matters."[47] The presence of error in ancient books can be expected; the initial false assumption of these scholars was that the Bible is like any other book. In other words, once they really examined what the Bible had to say, they found that their doubts faded and they became convinced of its historic, prophetic, and scientific accuracy. As Eastman and Missler conclude, considering modern scientific capabilities, "it can be demonstrated that the Bible is a skillfully designed, integrated message system that evidences supernatural engineering in every detail."[48]

When we examine biblical prophecy and mathematical probabilities, we find even more powerful evidence

---

* Wilder-Smith was the author of numerous popular and technical books and scientific papers, including *The Natural Sciences Know Nothing of Evolution*, *He Who Thinks Has to Believe*, and *The Creation of Life*.

that the Bible must be considered the Word of God. Think about it—God promised that predictions were 100-percent accurate and then offered 8,352 predictive verses in the Bible, including 1,817 total predictions with 737 separate matters forecast. Consider how unbelievably easy it would be to prove that the Bible is not the Word of God just by finding a single false prediction. But no false prediction has ever been proven.

When we consider just prophecy about the Messiah, we see that the odds against chance fulfillment are astronomical—literally impossible—and yet messianic prophecy is only a small part of the overall prophetic record in the Bible. The number of messianic predictions from which to choose is large: Authors variously discuss 73, 125-plus, and 400-plus.[49] Neither Jesus nor anyone else could have arranged to fulfill these prophecies. It is impossible for people to arrange such things as being born in a specific family; having your parents give birth to you in a specific town that is not their own city; specifying your own death with details beyond your ability to orchestrate, such as having yourself betrayed for an exact amount of money (30 pieces of silver) and having your executioners gamble for your clothes during your execution by crucifixion.

Peter Stoner, Professor Emeritus of Science at Westmont College, calculated the probability of one man fulfilling just eight major prophecies made concerning the Messiah. The estimates were worked out by 12 different classes of 600 college students. Stoner took their estimates and made them considerably more conservative. He encouraged skeptics or other scientists to make their own estimates to see if his conclusions were fair. Then he submitted his figures for review to a committee of the American Scientific Affiliation, which verified that his calculations "were accurate in regard to the scientific material presented."[50]

The very conservative chance of one man fulfilling all eight prophecies was 1 in 10^{17}, or 1 chance in 100 quadrillion (100,000,000,000,000,000.) In another calculation, Professor Stoner used 48 prophecies and arrived at the extremely conservative estimate that the probability is 1 in 10^{157} of 48 prophecies being fulfilled in one person[51]— for all practical purposes an infinitely larger figure than 1 chance in 10^{17}. In either case, we are dealing with the miraculous.

The immensity of the number 10^{157}

Imagine an ant. This ant has such severe arthritis it takes him 15 billion years just to travel *one inch*. His job is to carry a single atom on his back trillions and trillions of miles into space, and then return for one more atom. If he could carry only one atom at a time, how long would it take him to carry *all* the atoms in our universe trillions of miles into space?

Our little pain-ridden ant, even at his depressingly slow speed, could actually move *all* the atoms in our universe in 10^{157} years. Incidentally, just the atoms in the letters of this sentence number in the trillions and trillions, so you can imagine how long it would take him to carry just the atoms of this sentence, let alone an entire universe. But in 10^{157} years he could carry not just the atoms in *our* universe, but in 600,000 trillion, trillion, trillion, trillion universes like ours. And he could actually carry them a distance of 30 billion light-years—that is, endless trillions of miles into outer space, even to the known end of the universe and far, far beyond—*one atom at a time!*[52] That gives us a small idea of the immensity of the number 10^{157}.

Add to that immense impossibility the following information: As shown technically by Emile Borel and William Dembski, 1 "chance" in 10^{157} is actually no chance at all, ever. The probability is absolute zero.[53] Now, if no one in the world would bet their life savings on a horse race with winning odds of 1 chance in 1 million, why is it that so many people bet their convictions about reality—with far more sober consequences if wrong—on odds infinitely worse?

But enlarge the frame one more time. What of the 1,800 prophecies in the Bible, not just the 48 we've been considering? All this is proof that there must be a God who supernaturally gave this 100-percent correct information, and that he alone is the true God.

What can skeptics learn from prophecy, science, and mathematics about the Bible? Perhaps the most truthful and exciting declaration of all: *There is a God who can be known.*

The Responsibility of Historical Research

12

What is rationalistic biblical criticism, and how do we distinguish it from valid historical research?

Legitimate historical research attempts to be objective and reasonable, to be fair, to keep unwarranted speculation to a minimum, and to keep unjustified presuppositions from coloring the conclusions. On the other hand, rationalistic biblical criticism, also known as "higher" biblical criticism, such as form and redaction approaches, involves a particular attitude to the biblical text where unfounded assumptions and biases prevent a researcher from dealing fairly with biblical material. Presuppositions, of course, are not proven facts, and the philosophical, historical, or scientific assumptions underlying higher criticism are far from sound[1] (such as scientific naturalism, rationalism, and evolutionism).

Perhaps the most flawed basic assumption is that miracles are impossible, thus they never happen. If this assumption is true, then the Bible cannot be divinely inspired, for this would be a miracle. In addition, all the miracles recorded in the Bible, from Moses through the prophets to Jesus and the apostles, are obviously mythical or fraudulent since miracles never occur. And of course, Jesus never rose from the dead physically, so Christianity itself is based upon an immense deception, however well intended it might seem to be.

While there is clearly value to objective critical

research—especially textual criticism, which has vindicated the biblical text—inherently biased critical methods are of almost no historical value.

To illustrate, an article at www.infidels.org claimed to present a more balanced approach to biblical criticism and avoid the frequent biases one encounters. Yet in "Critique of New Testament Reliability and 'Bias' in NT Development," we find incredible statements. The author is as biased as anyone, allowing his premises to form his conclusions without looking reasonably at all the biblical, historical, and textual data. Without a shred of evidence he assumes there was a "Q" source (see below), that the Gospels cannot be fully reliable historically, and more: [2]

- "early Christians pictured Jesus as a magician"

- "the NT texts…changed so much over the centuries"

- "the gospels…are not firsthand accounts of his [Jesus'] deeds and activities"

- "All four of the gospels are pseudepigraphical works and today we use the names 'Matthew' or 'John' merely as convenient labels for the work"

- "the post-Easter Christ which is taught today is far different from the real wandering rabbi and Jewish peasant of first-century Palestine"

- "the Q material is present in nearly 200 verses in both Matthew and Luke"

Based on the facts we have, such conclusions are not only historically irresponsible, they are nonsense. And this is the problem of so much biblical "scholarship" today. It can be likened to a thirsty man finding a well of poisoned water in the desert—useless, disappointing, and dangerous all at once.

The above author is simply employing *radical form criticism*, beginning with the baseless premise that the biblical books make up a later and adulterated written form of oral teachings that had been circulated earlier. By the time this oral tradition was written down, say form critics, a great deal of deceptive alteration had occurred. Most of this deviation resulted from the inventive imagination of early Christians. In the end, form criticism concludes that most of what we find in the Bible is largely myth rather than history.

Redaction criticism builds directly upon radical form criticism. It is almost entirely a biased and subversive methodology. It assumes without any evidence that the findings of radical form criticism are legitimate and then extends the assumptions of Christian invention and myth even further. Redaction critics also attempt to uncover the theological *motivation* of an author, which leads to all sorts of irrelevant speculation.[3]

The biased or radical forms of literary, historical, and form criticism, plus redaction criticism, are often utilized together. The end result permits the critic or skeptic to sit in judgment on Scripture and, by whim and fancy alone, determine what he will or will not accept. Thus guesswork and individual bias dominate any investigation. The conclusion of these critical methodologies is that Christianity is a fraud, which allows us to make Jesus anyone we want him to be.

We suggested earlier that rationalistic critics and theologians generally, despite their claims, are not searchers after the truth. If they were, Jesus himself tells us they would *listen* to his words rather than discredit them.

For this reason I was born, and for this I came into the world, to testify to *the truth*. Everyone on the side of truth *listens to me* (John 18:37).

He also said, "I *am*...the truth" and "Your *word* is truth" (John 14:6; 17:17).

In the name of discovering truth, what we find is that the critics of the Bible are the real myth makers. We can know this because the conclusions drawn by higher criticism are *demonstrably false*, and yet they are broadcast far and wide and defended regardless. For example, it is logically impossible to believe the basic assumption of any criticism that, in effect, attributes to the scattered first-century Christian community the kind of creative power to fabricate the Jesus Christ of the New Testament. This is either unbelievable, absurd, or both:

> With regard to the discourses attributed to Jesus, it should at once be realized that a community cannot create such sayings. We know from experience that a saying must come originally from an individual. A community can only adopt, transmit, and preserve a saying, but the saying itself must first exist.
>
> Now the sayings attributed to Jesus in the gospels are by common consent of a singular nobility, loftiness, and power; elevated in character and style. If it be held that in some way the Christian community originated these discourses and statements, then it must follow, as scholar Burton Scott Easton argues, that the Palestinian church either had in its midst a single, brilliant thinker "from whom the sayings all proceeded, but whose name and very existence has disappeared from history—something well-nigh unthinkable—or else there were a number of gifted individuals all fired with the same superlative genius and all endowed with the same exquisite style—an even more difficult conception."

The simple fact is that there is not the slightest indication in New Testament or secular history of the existence of such an anonymous, dynamic, prophetic leader, who would surely be greater and wiser even than ancient Solomon; or of a group of such leaders, gifted with the capacity of creating original discourses such as are found in the gospels. The only plausible explanation for these sayings is that they originated, as the evangelists declare, with Jesus; the life situation from which they stem is assuredly to be found in Jesus Himself.[4]

Indeed, the more we carefully examine negative criticism as a whole, the more difficult it is to accept its conclusions. It reminds us of the situation with the naturalistic explanations for the origin of the universe and life or for the physical resurrection of Christ—all of these are much harder to believe than the miracle of creation or the resurrection itself.

An actual and compelling event

Given the Jewish origin of Christianity, only Christ's resurrection could have provided the stimulus for Christian beginnings, because Jesus' teachings would have been proven fraudulent unless he rose physically from the dead; his followers would have continued their abandonment of him. The first 25,000 or so Christians were all Jews who, based exclusively on Christ's resurrection, radically revised sacred and inviolate Jewish institutions—for example, discarding animal sacrifice, eliminating legalistic keeping of the Sabbath, which actually changed to Sunday, rejecting the Mosaic Law as a means of salvation, a theology of Unitarian monotheism altered to Trinitarianism, and so on. Such powerful and immutable institutions could never have been revised *by Jews* apart from the resurrection of their messiah, Jesus.

In similar fashion, critical approaches and their logical conclusions are far more difficult to believe than what the New Testament plainly teaches. If what the critics say were true, there never would have been a religion of Christianity to begin with.[5] The mere fact that Christianity exists is disproof of the critics' theories. In the end, our only options are to believe in 1) the folly of a critical methodology and its myths or 2) the soundness of what the Bible teaches. Proof of this is further illustrated in the next question.

13

Are rationalistic critical approaches such as the Jesus Seminar and "Q" studies nothing more than nonsense?

As we have already seen, critical theories encompass numerous historic errors, internal contradictions, reversals of position, blatant ignoring of contrary data, special pleading, and so on. When, upon the flimsiest of grounds, critics reject the Bible, which Jesus authenticated on unassailable grounds, they only reveal their own misunderstanding. Somehow they assume they are wiser than Jesus. For hundreds of years in biblical studies, scholars have spent little time questioning the frailty of their own assumptions.

The strange case of the Jesus Seminar

The Jesus Seminar aptly illustrates the unfortunate methods of liberal critical biblical scholarship generally. In 1993, the conclusions of the Jesus Seminar were published in a large, detailed text titled *The Five Gospels: The Search for the Authentic Words of Jesus*. This volume reduces Jesus' fully authentic words in the Gospels to *less than six percent* of what is recorded. In other words, these scholars say, 94 percent of what we read Jesus saying in the Gospels has some degree of doubt attached to it or is just plain wrong.

More specifically, "Eighty-two percent of the words ascribed to Jesus in the gospels were not actually spoken by him."[6] In the Gospel of Mark, for example, the Seminar deemed only one single verse out of over 280 verses as definitely spoken by Jesus—Mark 12:17. This means that Mark (or, supposedly, Christian tradition) misquoted or invented the words of Jesus some 300 times for every time he quoted Jesus correctly. And worse, virtually *everything* in the Gospel of John was voted unreliable. This is scholarly prejudice taken to the point of absurdity.

Let us now examine three of the many key errors made by the Jesus Seminar:

1. *The false claim of consensus.* The Seminar maintains that its conclusions represent a consensus of modern scholarship. However, the views of 70 radically biased rationalistic critics cannot be considered representative of the 7,000 members of the Society of Biblical Literature (SBL), not to mention thousands of others.

2. *Its deliberate skepticism and prejudice.* Entirely without justification is the Seminar's premeditated agenda to discredit people's trust in the Gospels *despite* their being established as historically reliable. We read with astonishment this declaration:

> The evidence provided by the written gospels is hearsay evidence. Hearsay evidence is secondhand evidence… none of them [the Gospel authors] was an ear or eyewitness of the words and events he records. [7]

Now if you arbitrarily discard the great majority of the Gospels as unreliable, you are unlikely to credit anyone's claims to being an eyewitness, such as those of the apostle John, first in his Gospel (21:24), and then in his first epistle:

> That which was from the beginning, which we have heard, which we have seen with our eyes, which we have looked at and our hands have touched—this we proclaim…We proclaim to you what we have seen and heard (1 John 1:1,3).

Indeed, in the Gospel of John, the noun "witness" or "testimony" and the verb "testify" are used almost 50 times.* No wonder the Jesus Seminar so thoroughly discarded it.

3. *Serious or fatal methodological flaws.* The Seminar's faulty methods tear down its own premises and conclusions—such as their naturalistic bias and hostility toward biblical faith. For example, the Seminar's claims to impartiality and the use of legal standards of evidence are highly misleading. The truth is, their "rules" of investigation are frequently irrelevant, or else they incorporate their own biases against the text so that *applying* the rules only proves the critical conclusions already held. Thus, their context rule assumes without justification that the Gospel writers "*invent[ed]* new narrative contexts" for the sayings of Jesus.[8] Or, for example:

> The Christ creed and dogma…can no longer command the assent of those who have seen the heavens

---

* Luke 1:2; 24:48; Hebrews 2:3; 1 Peter 5:1; John 3:11; 5:36; 19:35; 21:24; Acts 2:32; 3:15; 5:32; 10:39; 26:26; 1 John 4:14; 5:9-10.

through Galileo's telescope. The old deities and demons were swept from the skies…[Science has] dismantled the mythological abodes of the gods and Satan, and bequeathed us secular heavens.[9]

And when the Seminar disparages conservative Christians as "far-right fundamentalists," "latter-day inquisitors," and "witch-hunters" and then claims "their reading of who Jesus was rests on the shifting sands of their own theological constructions," their prejudices stand fully exposed.[10] Unfortunately, the scholars of the Jesus Seminar care little for objective historical inquiry concerning the Gospels.

The "Q" fantasy

To illustrate more untamed speculation based on microscopic evidence, consider the collection of nonexistent Jesus sayings termed "Q" (supposedly used by Matthew, Mark, and Luke). Liberal scholars such as Burton Mack in *Who Wrote the New Testament?: The Making of the Christian Myth* (1995) are now speaking even of Q1, Q2, Q3, and Q4. As theologian Craig Blomberg points out, this is preposterous; and it explains "why so much of contemporary New Testament scholarship is viewed with derision by mainstream historians. The entire edifice is 'a house of cards'…Pull out one element and the whole construction crumbles."[11]

John Wenham, a distinguished author and academician we have quoted earlier, illustrates the quandary of biased critics. Wenham quotes M.D. Goulder, who asserts, "Not tens but hundreds of thousands of pages have been wasted by authors on this Synoptic Problem [that is, the likenesses and differences between the first three gospels] by not paying attention to errors of method." Wenham goes on to comment that "much of the argumentation is worth very little, because so many of the arguments are reversible: they can be argued either way with approximately equal cogency."[12]

Thus, "Q" illustrates the problem scholars get themselves into when they are unwilling to take the text at face value even though there is every reason to do so. Again, "Q" doesn't even *exist*, yet literally millions of research hours have been consumed dissecting it! This is illustrated in the International "Q" Project's database of research, which contains, for example, a 90-page single-spaced analysis of a *single* verse from Matthew—which was ultimately decided *not* to be "Q"![13]

Why emphasize the detailed study of something that doesn't exist, when what *does* exist is both authentic and accurate, not to mention vital? Nonetheless, the "Q" project intends to publish more than 60 300-page volumes painstakingly evaluating its make-believe text! Each 300-page volume will deal with about 100 "words" from "Q"; that's three pages of scholarly analysis and discussion for every nonexistent word of "Q."[14]

Critics demand we reject as myth the "inventive imaginations" of the early Christians in regard to Jesus, but then they turn around and demand we accept their own conjured reconstructions as literal "gospel." (No double standard here.) John Wenham points out one of the central problems with "Q":

> When we try to put the Q-theory to the test the matter is of course complicated by the fact that we have no text of Q to work with…S. Petrie in his *Novum Testamentum* 3 (1959) article, " 'Q' is Only What You Make It" has shown this in a colourful way. He speaks of the "exasperating contradictoriness" of scholarly views as to its nature:

"Q" is a single document; it is a composite document, incorporating earlier sources; it is used in different redactions; it is more than one document. The original language of "Q" is Greek; the original language is Aramaic; it is used in different translations. "Q" is the Matthean Logia; it is not the Matthean Logia. "Q" has a definite shape; it is no more than an amorphous collection of fragments. "Q" is a gospel; it is not a gospel. "Q" includes the Crucifixion story; it does not include the Crucifixion story. "Q" consists wholly of sayings and there is no narrative; it includes some narrative. All of "Q" is preserved in Matt. and Luke; not all of it is preserved; it is better preserved in Luke. Matt.'s order is the correct order; Luke's is the correct order; neither order is correct. "Q" is used by Mark; it is not used by Mark.[15]

It seems clear that critical scholars have used inventive theories like "Q" simply to make Jesus into an image they are comfortable with—whether political revolutionary, mistaken Jewish sage, mystic, cynic, protofeminist, and so on. Thus, Jesus' death and resurrection play no role in "Q's" understanding of salvation, which is clearly more gnostic than biblical. And of course, "Q" has been appropriated by the Jesus Seminar "in their ongoing enterprise of 'dismantling the church's canon.'"[16] As Burton Mack argues,

> The remarkable thing about the people of Q is that they were not Christians. They did not think of Jesus as a Messiah. They did not regard his death as a...saving event...they did not imagine that he had been raised from the dead.[17]

It seems that any and every image of Jesus is currently acceptable to critics—except the one in the New

Testament. Given the stated goal of discrediting orthodox Christianity, such a hopeless state of affairs is not surprising.

The reason for the critical conclusions should be obvious: If we accept the actual Jesus of history, the Jesus of the New Testament, then he is not only our Lord and Savior but our final Judge as well. He is not someone we may trifle with, but the One we must bow to as our Sovereign. We may sit in judgment upon him now, but apart from repentance, it is he who will sit in judgment upon us later. Since the human heart, in its rebellion, prefers any thought but this, the almost desperate nature of the "scholarship" to formulate a new Jesus is understandable. After all, once the biblical Jesus is adequately "disposed" of, we need not worry about the present or the future.

Matters of life and death

Lest we think this is all just academic debating, consider the tragic event relayed by William Lane Craig in *The Son Rises,* his text on the historical evidence for Christ's physical resurrection from the dead. He recalls the incident of a retired pastor "who in his spare time began to study the thought of certain modern theologians." This pastor believed that their great learning was superior to his own and concluded that their views must be correct. "He understood clearly what that meant for him: His whole life and ministry had been based on a bundle of lies. He committed suicide."

Dr. Craig comments, appropriately, "I believe that modern theologians must answer to God for that man's death. One cannot make statements on such matters without accepting part of the responsibility for the consequences."[18]

We are not overstating it when we say that these are life and death issues…If Jesus is who he claimed to be and who his followers declare him to be, then we are not dealing simply with academic questions. We are instead dealing with the most important questions of the modern person's daily life and eternal destiny."[19]

The unflattering truth about liberal theologians and other unrepentant skeptics is that they are, unfortunately, enemies of the cross of Christ and of people's hope for salvation. As the apostle Paul warned,

As I have often told you before and now say again even with tears, many live as enemies of the cross of Christ. Their destiny is destruction, their god is their stomach, and their glory is in their shame (Philippians 3:18-19).

Conclusion

14

How unique is the Bible?

In asking the questions that need to be addressed to find one's purpose in life, a person is inevitably drawn to the Bible, as countless millions have been before. In simple chart form below is concise information about the Bible that readers should weigh as they consider life, their place in the universe, and what God may offer to and require of them. But the key message of the Bible can be summed up even more concisely:

> God so loved the world that He gave His only begotten Son, that whoever believes in Him shall not perish, but have eternal life (John 3:16 NASB).

As Jesus emphasized, "This is eternal life: that they may know you, the only true God, and Jesus Christ, whom you have sent" (John 17:3). If you want to know God personally, you can begin by saying the following prayer to him:

> *Dear God: I confess my sin and turn from it. I ask Jesus Christ to enter my life and to become my Lord and Savior. I recognize this is a solemn decision that you take very seriously. I believe that on the cross Jesus Christ died for my sin, and I receive him into my life now. My commitment to you is that I will follow him, and I will trust you to give me the strength for this. In Jesus' name, amen.*

The uniqueness of the Bible

1. The Bible is the only book in the world that offers objective evidence that it is the Word of God. Only the Bible gives real proof of its divine inspiration.

2. The Bible is the only religious scripture in the world that is inerrant.

3. Only the Bible has unique theological content; for example, it is the only religious scripture that offers eternal salvation as a free gift entirely by God's grace simply through belief in Jesus.

4. Only the Bible provides historical proof that the one true God sacrificially loves mankind.

5. The Bible contains the greatest moral standards of any book.

6. Only the Bible begins with the creation of the universe by divine fiat and contains a continuous, though often brief and interspersed, historical record of mankind from the first man, Adam, to the end of history.

7. Only the Bible contains detailed prophecies about the coming Savior of the world—prophecies that have proven true in history.

8. Only the Bible has a completely realistic view of human nature; the power to convict people of their sin; the ability to change human nature; and the realistic offer of a permanent solution to the problem of human sin and evil.

9. The Bible is the only ancient book with documented scientific and medical prevision. No other ancient book is ever carefully analyzed along scientific lines, but many books have been written on the theme of the Bible and modern science.

10. Of all religious scriptures, only the Bible has its accuracy confirmed in history by archaeology.

11. The internal and historical characteristics of the Bible are unique in their unity and internal consistency; despite the Bible's production over a 1500-year period by 40-plus authors writing in several nations and discussing scores of controversial subjects, there is nonetheless agreement on all issues.

12. The Bible is the most translated, purchased, memorized, and persecuted book in history.

13. Only the Bible is fully one-quarter prophetic; the typical English Bible contains some 400 complete pages of predictions.

14. Only the Bible has withstood 2,000 years of intense scrutiny by critics, not only surviving the attacks but prospering and having its credibility strengthened by such criticism.*

15. The Bible has had more influence in the world than any other book.

16. Only the Bible has a person-specific (Christ-centered) nature for each of its 66 books, detailing that person's life in prophecy, type, antitype, and so on, from 400 to 1500 years before that person was born.

17. Only the Bible proclaims a resurrection of its central figure that is proven in history.

18. The Bible is the only major ancient religious Scripture whose textual preservation is established as virtually autographic (identical to the original manuscripts).

19. The Bible is uniquely distinguished in its content. Where else can you find anything like the history of the Pentateuch, the lessons of Job, the message and heroism of the prophets of Israel, the miracles of the book of Esther, the drama of the books of Kings and Chronicles, the praise and comfort of the Psalms, the wisdom of Proverbs and Ecclesiastes, the amazing prophecies of Daniel, the matchless life of Jesus, the deep theology of Galatians and Romans, or the sweeping conclusion of Revelation—all in one book, with eternal promises throughout?

Learning from History

If many of the greatest persons who have ever lived have made declarations such as those listed below, should not we conclude that the Bible is worthy of our personal commitment to learning its teachings? The Christian church has a marvelous treasure, and

---

* Voltaire (1694–1778) predicted the Bible would be extinct within a century; within half a century Voltaire was dead, and his house was a warehouse of Bibles for the Geneva Bible Society.

presenting it to and honoring it before the world is one of its greatest privileges.

But let us ask, when was the last time you read your Bible? Have you seriously and systematically attempted to learn its teachings? Have you tried to apply these teachings in your own life? If men and women of such caliber as those below have thought the Bible was so very important, and if it is *indeed* the Word of God Almighty, can we do anything else but apply it—and should this not become our first priority? In the end, is anything more important?

Consider the words of Blanche Mary Kelly—the Bible is "the most stupendous book, the most sublime literature, even apart from its sacred character, in the history of the world." Or those of E.S. Bates: "No individual, no Caesar or Napoleon, has had such a part in the world's history as this book."

Considering the influence of the Bible, the *Encyclopedia Britannica* tells us that it has

> played a special role in the history and culture of the modern world…The Bible brought its view of God, the universe, and mankind into all the leading Western languages and thus into the intellectual processes of Western man…the Bible…has been the most available, familiar, and dependable source and arbiter of intellectual, moral, and spiritual ideals in the West. Millions of modern people who do not think of themselves as religious live nevertheless with basic presuppositions that underlie biblical literature. It would be impossible to calculate the effect of such presuppositions on the changing ideas and attitudes of Western people with regard to the nature and purpose of government, social institutions, and economic theories.[1]

In *Books That Changed the World*, Robert B. Downs, former president of the American Library Association, wrote,

> The Bible has exercised a more profound and contin-
> uous influence upon Western civilization than has any
> other literary work. To consider only one phase, bib-
> lical language, style, and content pervade the writings
> of countless poets, dramatists, and other authors. The
> jurisprudence and customs of the West have been shaped
> by the legal and ethical precepts of the Bible. Even more
> fundamental, its deep insights into the motives of human
> nature and conduct, the tragedy of man's earthly destiny,
> and the search "for a better country, that is, an heavenly"
> have throughout the centuries directed human faith,
> thought, behavior, and endeavor.[2]

Note what Keith Schoville, a scholar in Hebrew and Semitic studies, has to say about the Bible:

> The Bible, as a religious work, needs no proof of its inspi-
> ration and authenticity. Its truth is timeless and eternally
> valid, one evidence of which is its continuing influence
> on world culture right down to the twentieth century…
> Thus far, no historical statement in the Bible has ever
> been proved false on the basis of evidence retrieved
> through archeological research.[3]

Finally, consider some brief statements of the famous and influential.[4] We challenge anyone to read these short citations by some of the most significant people in history and not be impressed.

> *Abraham Lincoln:* "This great book…is the best gift God
> has given to man."

Ulysses S. Grant: "To the influence of this book we are indebted for the progress made in civilization, and to this we must look as our guide in the future."

Woodrow Wilson: "A man has found himself when he has found his relation to the rest of the universe, and here is the Book in which those relations are set forth."

John Quincy Adams: "Great is my veneration for the Bible."

Sir Isaac Newton: "There are more sure marks of authenticity in the Bible than in any profane history." "I account the Scriptures of God the most sublime philosophy."

Galileo: "I believe that the intention of Holy Writ was to persuade men of the truths necessary to salvation."

Cecil B. DeMille: "After more than 60 years of almost daily reading of the Bible, I never fail to find it always new and marvelously in tune with the changing needs of every day."

Johann Wolfgang von Goethe: "The Bible becomes ever more beautiful the more it is understood."

Immanuel Kant: "The Bible is the greatest benefit which the human race has ever experienced."

Charles Dickens: "The New Testament is the best book the world has ever known or will know."

Jean-Jacques Rousseau: "I must confess to you that the majesty of the Scriptures astonishes me."

Patrick Henry: "There is a Book worth all other books which were ever printed."

William E. Gladstone: "The Bible was stamped with speciality of origin, and an immeasurable distance separates it from all competitors."

Sir William Blackstone: "The Bible has always been regarded as part of the Common Law of England."

Queen Victoria: "England has become great and happy by the knowledge of the true God through Jesus Christ… This is the secret of England's greatness."

Mark Twain: "It is hard to make a choice of the most beautiful passage in a Book which is gemmed with beautiful passages as the Bible."

Alexander Hamilton: "I have carefully examined the evidences of the Christian religion, and if I were sitting as a juror upon its authenticity, I would unhesitatingly give my verdict in its favor."

Thomas Huxley: "The Bible has been the Magna Carta of the poor and the oppressed. The human race is not in a position to dispense with it."

Horace Greeley: "It is impossible to enslave mentally or socially a Bible-reading people. The principles of the Bible are the groundwork of human freedom."

Robert E. Lee: "In all my perplexities and distresses, the Bible has never failed to give me light and strength."

Alfred, Lord Tennyson: "Bible reading is an education in itself."

Thomas Jefferson: "The studious perusal of the sacred volume will make better citizens, better fathers, and better husbands."

Samuel Taylor Coleridge: "For more than a thousand years, the Bible, collectively taken, has gone hand in hand with civilization, science, law—in short, with the moral and intellectual cultivation of the species, always supporting and leading the way."

John Locke: "The Bible is one of the greatest blessings bestowed by God on the children of man."

Roger Bacon: "I wish to show that there is one wisdom which is perfect, and that this is contained in the Scriptures."

William Lyon Phelps: "Western civilization is founded upon the Bible; all our ideas, our wisdom, our philosophy, our literature, our art, our ideals come more from the Bible than all other books put together."

RECOMMENDED RESOURCES

Books

The Encyclopedia of Bible Difficulties, Gleason L. Archer Jr.

The Historical Reliability of the Gospels, Craig L. Blomberg

How to Read a Book, Mortimer Adler

How to Read the Bible for All Its Worth: A Guide to Understanding the Bible,
   Gordon Fee and Douglas Stuart

The New Testament Documents: Are They Reliable? F.F. Bruce

The Old Testament Documents: Are They Reliable and Relevant? Walter C.
   Kaiser Jr.

On the Reliability of the Old Testament, K.A. Kitchen

A Survey of Old Testament Introduction, Gleason L. Archer Jr.

Under the Influence: How Christianity Transformed Civilization, Alvin J.
   Schmidt

What if the Bible Had Never Been Written? D. James Kennedy and Jerry
   Newcombe

Why Good Arguments Often Fail: Making a More Persuasive Case for Christ,
   James W. Sire

Internet

www.Bible.org

www.BibleGateway.com

www.BibleLiteracy.org

www.JohnAnkerberg.org

www.WallBuilders.com

www.WalterMartin.org/links

NOTES

Section One—The Bible and the Difference It Makes

1. Johnson's paper can be found at www.leaderu.com/truth/1truth08.html.

2. See Paul Kengor, *God and Ronald Reagan* (New York: Harper Perennial, 2005).

3. Aldous Huxley, *Ends and Means* (London: Chatto & Windus, 1946), p. 270.

4. Original inerrancy is integrally related to both the doctrine of inspiration and the nature of God. First, the biblical doctrine of inspiration is taught to be verbal and plenary, that is, involving the very words (Matthew 4:4) and extending to every part of Scripture (2 Timothy 3:16). If God is incapable of inspiring error, whatever is inspired must be inerrant.

Second, just as the Bible reveals God's nature is holy and righteous (that is, he is incapable of lying), it also reveals that he is omnipotent. Because his inspiration extends to every word, it is incapable of error, and because God is omnipotent, he can safeguard the process of inspiration from error, even though it is given through fallible men. The term "the Lord says" or similar expressions are used some 2,800 times in the Old Testament (Isaiah 40:8; Jeremiah 1:11; cf. Deuteronomy 18:18; 1 Kings 22:14; Amos 3:1; Exodus 34:27; Jeremiah 36:27-28; Isaiah 8:19). Inspiration (involving inerrancy) is explicitly asserted for nearly 70 percent of the Old Testament (26 of 39 books). In addition, "Twenty of twenty-two Old Testament books [or 90 percent] have their authority and/or authenticity directly affirmed by the New Testament" (Norman L. Geisler and William E. Nix, *A General Introduction to the Bible* [Chicago: Moody Press, 1971], p. 87).

But God also preauthenticated the inspiration of the New Testament. In promising the disciples that the Holy Spirit would teach them all things and bring to remembrance the things Jesus taught them (John 14:26, referring in part to the Gospels, cf. Matthew 24:35) and that the Holy Spirit would guide them into all the truth (John 16:13-15, referring in part to the remainder of the New Testament), it is not surprising that "virtually every New Testament writer claimed that his writing was divinely authoritative…The cumulative effect of this self-testimony is an overwhelming confirmation that the New Testament writers claimed inspiration" (Geisler and Nix, pp. 91, 97). Some examples of New Testament claims for the inspiration include 2 Timothy 3:16; 2 Peter 1:20-21; 3:2,15-16; Revelation 1:1-3; 22:18-19; and 1 Thessalonians 4:9.

5. Paul D. Feinberg, "The Meaning of Inerrancy," in Norman L. Geisler, ed., *Inerrancy* (Grand Rapids, MI: The Zondervan Corporation, 1979, 1980), p. 294.

6. For example, inerrancy does not require strict scientific, technical, grammatical, semantic, numeric, or historic precision. For instance, to speak of a "setting sun" is not error in spite of its scientific imprecision; and September 14, 15, or 16 (or all taken together) is, properly, the middle of the month of September. Inerrancy

does not demand verbatim exactness when the New Testament quotes the Old, assuming a New Testament quotation does not contradict an Old Testament one, nor does it require that any given biblical event be exhaustively reported.

7. John Murray, "The Attestation of Scripture" in N.B. Stonehouse and Paul Woolley, eds., *The Infallible Word: A Symposium*, 3rd ed., rev. (Grand Rapids, MI: Baker Book House, 1967), pp. 26-27.

8. Critical defenses of inerrancy have been successfully argued by numerous scholars. See R.C. Sproul, "The Case for Inerrancy: A Methodological Analysis," in John Warwick Montgomery, ed., *God's Inerrant Word* (Minneapolis, MN: Bethany, 1974), pp. 242-262; John Warwick Montgomery, *The Shape of the Past* (Minneapolis, MN: Bethany, 1975), pp. 138-152; Charles Feinberg in Geisler, ed., *Inerrancy*, pp. 269-287; also Warfield; Arthur Holmes in Geisler, ed., *Inerrancy*; and J.I. Packer, *Beyond the Battle for the Bible* (Westchester, IL: Cornerstone Books, 1980). See also Geisler's comments in Geisler, ed., *Inerrancy*, p. 242, who sees some validity in each approach—inductive, deductive, adductive, and retroductive.

9. Following the arguments of Montgomery and Sproul in Montgomery, *Shape of the Past*, pp. 138-139; R.C. Sproul, "The Case for Inerrancy: A Methodological Analysis," in Montgomery, *God's Inerrant Word*, p. 248, cf., 248-260.

10. John Wenham, *Christ and the Bible* (Downers Grove, IL: InterVarsity, 1973), chaps. 1–2, 5. See also Wenham's chapter in Geisler, ed., *Inerrancy*, pp. 3-38; Benjamin B. Warfield, *The Inspiration and Authority of the Bible*; Pierre Ch. Marcel, "Our Lord's Use of Scripture," in Carl F.H. Henry, ed., *Revelation and the Bible* (Grand Rapids, MI: Baker, 1969), pp. 119-134; and René Pache, *The Inspiration and Authority of Scripture* (Chicago: Moody Press, 1966), chap. 18.

11. John Warwick Montgomery, "Biblical Inerrancy: What Is at Stake?" in Montgomery, ed., *God's Inerrant Word*, p. 38. For more about Montgomery's intellectual legacy, see the forthcoming book *Tough-Minded Christianity: Legacy of John Warwick Montgomery* (Nashville, TN: B&H Academic, 2009).

Section Two—The Accuracy and Supernatural Character of the Biblical Text

1. See www.RonRhodes.org/Manuscript.html.

2. See www.RonRhodes.org/Manuscript.html; see also Randall Price, *Searching for the Original Bible* (Eugene, OR: Harvest House Publishers, 2007).

3. Adapted from www.RonRhodes.org/Manuscript.html.

4. Josh McDowell, *Evidence That Demands a Verdict* (San Bernardino, CA: Campus Crusade for Christ, 1969), p. 42; Robert C. Newman, "Miracles and the Historicity of the Easter Week Narratives," in John Warwick Montgomery, ed., *Evidence for Faith: Deciding the God Question* (Dallas: Word, 1991), pp. 281-284.

5. Norman L. Geisler and William E. Nix, *A General Introduction to the Bible* (Chicago: Moody Press, 1971), pp. 238-239; 365-366; cf., McDowell, *Evidence*, pp. 43-45.

6. McDowell, *Evidence*, pp. 43-45; Clark Pinnock, *Biblical Revelation: The Foundation of Christian Theology* (Chicago: Moody Press, 1971), pp. 238-239, 365-366.

7. William M. Ramsay, *The Bearing of Recent Discovery on the Trustworthiness of the New Testament* (Grand Rapids, MI: Baker, 1959), p. 81; A.N. Sherwin-White, *Roman Society and Roman Law in the New Testament* (Oxford: Clarendon Press,

1963), as cited in Norman L. Geisler, *Christian Apologetics* (Grand Rapids, MI: Baker, 1976), p. 326.

8. McDowell, *Evidence*, pp. 39-52; Geisler and Nix, pp. 238, 357-367.

9. Gary Habermas, *Ancient Evidence for the Life of Jesus* (Nashville, TN: Thomas Nelson, 1973), pp. 112-115; cf. F.F. Bruce, *The New Testament Documents: Are They Reliable?* (Downers Grove, IL: InterVarsity, 1971), chaps. 9-10.

10. John Wenham, *Redating Matthew, Mark and Luke* (Downers Grove, IL: Inter-Varsity, 1992), pp. 115-119, 136, 183, see pp. xxv, 147, 198, 200, 221, 223, 238-239, 243-245.

11. John A.T. Robinson, *Redating the New Testament* (Philadelphia: Westminster, 1976).

12. Cf. Wenham, p. 200.

13. F.F. Bruce, "Are the New Testament Documents Still Reliable?" in *Christianity Today*, October 28, 1978, p. 33.

14. For example, Gerhard Meier, *The End of the Historical Critical Method* (St. Louis, MO: Concordia, 1977) and Josh McDowell, *More Evidence That Demands a Verdict* (San Bernardino, CA: Campus Crusade for Christ, 1972).

15. For examples, see our *Handbook of Biblical Evidences* (Eugene, OR: Harvest House, 2008), pp. 86-94.

16. See J.W. Montgomery, *The Law Above the Law* (Minneapolis, MN: Bethany, 1975), appendix reproducing this work, pp. 91-140.

17. Reproduced in *The Simon Greenleaf Law Review*, vol. 1 (Orange, CA: The Faculty of the Simon Greenleaf School of Law, 1981–1982), pp. 15-74.

18. Irwin Linton, *A Lawyer Examines the Bible* (San Diego: Creation-Life-Publishers, 1977), p. 45.

19. Montgomery, *The Law Above the Law*, pp. 87-88.

20. Norman Geisler, *Christ: The Theme of the Bible* (Chicago: Moody Press, 1969), n29, citing D.J. Wiseman, "Archaeological Confirmations of the Old Testament," in Carl F. Henry, ed., *Revelation and the Bible* (Grand Rapids, MI: Baker, 1958), pp. 301-302.

21. E.M. Blaiklock, "Editor's Preface," *The New International Dictionary of Biblical Archaeology* (Grand Rapids, MI: Regency Reference Library/Zondervan, 1983), pp. vii-viii, emphasis added.

22. J.A. Thompson, *The Bible and Archaeology* (Grand Rapids, MI: Eerdmans, 1975), p. 5; Norman Geisler and Ron Brooks, *When Skeptics Ask: A Handbook on Christian Evidences* (Wheaton, IL: Victor, 1990), p. 200.

23. Geisler and Brooks, p. 200; John Warwick Montgomery, "The Jury Returns: A Juridical Defense of Christianity," in Montgomery, ed., *Evidence for Faith*, p. 326.

24. W.F. Albright, *The Archaeology of Palestine*, rev. ed. (Pelican Books, 1960), p. 127.

25. Nelson Glueck, as quoted in Keith N. Schoville, *Biblical Archaeology in Focus* (Grand Rapids, MI: Baker, 1978), p. 163; cf., Geisler and Brooks, p. 179.

26. Clifford Wilson, *Archaeology, the Bible and Christ* (Pacific Christian Ministries, PO Box 311, Lilydale 3140, Victoria, Australia), vol. 17, p. 62.

27. As cited in McDowell, *Evidence*, p. 66.

28. E.M. Blaiklock, *Christianity Today*, September 28, 1973, p. 13.

29. For example, Edwin Yamauchi, *The Stone and the Scriptures* (New York: J.B. Lippincott, 1972), pp. 30,161.

30. Joseph P. Free, rev. and exp. Howard F. Vos, *Archaeology and Bible History* (Grand Rapids: Zondervan, 1992), pp. 255-257.

31. Cf. Craig L. Blomberg, "Where Do We Start Studying Jesus?" in Michael J. Wilkins and J.P. Moreland, eds., *Jesus Under Fire: Modern Scholarship Reinvents the Historical Jesus* (Grand Rapids, MI: Zondervan, 1995), p. 221.

32. W. Arndt, *Does the Bible Contradict Itself?: A Discussion of Alleged Contradictions in the Bible*, 5th ed. rev. (St. Louis, MO: Concordia, 1955); John W. Haley, *Alleged Discrepancies of the Bible* (Grand Rapids, MI: Baker, rpt. 1982); Gleason Archer, *The Encyclopedia of Bible Difficulties* (Grand Rapids, MI: Zondervan, 1982).

33. For example, Gleason L. Archer Jr., *A Survey of Old Testament Introduction*, rev. ed. (Chicago, IL: Moody Press, 1974); Josh McDowell, *Daniel in the Critic's Den* (San Bernardino, CA: Campus Crusade for Christ, 1973); R.D. Wilson, *Studies in the Book of Daniel*, 2 vols. rpt. (Grand Rapids, MI: Baker, 1979); see "Bible Criticism," in Norman Geisler, *Baker Encyclopedia of Christian Apologetics* (Grand Rapids, MI: Baker, 1999).

34. K.A. Kitchen, *Ancient Orient and Old Testament* (Chicago: InterVarsity Press, 1973), p. 23, first emphasis added.

35. John Warwick Montgomery, *The Shape of the Past* (Minneapolis, MN: Bethany, 1975), p. 176.

36. Archer, *Encyclopedia of Bible Difficulties*, pp. 11-12.

37. Arndt, p. xi.

38. J. Barton Payne, *Encyclopedia of Biblical Prophecy: The Complete Guide to Scriptural Predictions and Their Fulfillment* (New York: Harper & Row, 1973), p. 13.

39. John Wesley White, *Re-Entry* (Grand Rapids, MI: Zondervan, 1971), p. 14; cf. p. 680.

40. See John MacArthur, *The Second Coming: Signs of Christ's Return and the End of the Age* (Wheaton, IL: Crossway, 2003).

41. Archer, *Survey of Old Testament Introduction*, pp. 326-351.

42. See McDowell, *Daniel*; John Walvoord, *Daniel: The Key to Prophetic Revelation* (Chicago: Moody, 1972).

43. Adapted from Geisler and Brooks, pp. 114-115.

44. A good place to start is Os Guinness, *God in the Dark: The Assurance of Faith Beyond a Shadow of Doubt* (Wheaton, IL: Crossway, 1996).

45. Mark Eastman and Chuck Missler, *The Creator Beyond Time and Space* (Costa Mesa, CA: The Word for Today, 1996), pp. 23, 87.

46. Eastman and Missler, p. 101.

47. A.E. Wilder-Smith, *The Reliability of the Bible* (San Diego: Master Books, 1983), p. 39.

48. Eastman and Missler, p. 101.

49. See respectively, James Smith, *What the Bible Teaches About the Promised Messiah* (Nashville, TN: Nelson, 1993); Payne, *Encyclopedia of Biblical Prophecy*;

Alfred Edersheim, *The Life and Times of Jesus the Messiah* (Grand Rapids, MI: Eerdmans, 1972).

50. Peter W. Stoner, *Science Speaks: Scientific Proof of the Accuracy of Prophecy and the Bible* (Chicago: Moody Press, 1969), p. 4.

51. Stoner, p. 109.

52. Adapted from James Coppedge, *Evolution: Possible or Impossible?* (Grand Rapids, MI: Zondervan, 1973), p. 120.

53. Emile Borel, *Probabilities and Life* (New York: Dover, 1962), chaps. 1 and 3; Borel's cosmic limit of 10^{200} changes nothing in this calculation. See the improvement in Borel's law, Dembski's "Law of Small Probability"—"Specified events of small probability do not occur by chance"—in William A. Dembski, *The Design Inference* (New York: Cambridge University Press, 1998), pp. 2-9. "In eliminating chance, the design inference eliminates not just a single chance hypothesis, but all relevant chance hypotheses" (Dembski, p. 8).

Section Three—The Responsibility of Historical Research

1. J.P. Moreland, ed., *The Creation Hypothesis: Scientific Evidence for an Intelligent Designer* (Downers Grove, IL: InterVarsity Press, 1994); Michael Wilkins and J.P. Moreland, *Jesus Under Fire: Modern Scholarship Reinvents the Historical Jesus* (Downers Grove, IL: InterVarsity, 1995).

2. James Still, "Critique of New Testament Reliability and 'Bias' in NT Development," www.infidels.org.

3. See Walter Maier, *Form Criticism Reexamined* (St. Louis, MO: Concordia Publishing House, 1973), pp. 7-10.

4. Maier, p. 38.

5. We demonstrated this in Ankerberg and Weldon, *Handbook of Biblical Evidence* (Eugene, OR: Harvest House Publishers, 2008), pp. 82-86.

6. Robert W. Funk, Roy W. Hoover, and the Jesus Seminar, *The Five Gospels: The Search for the Authentic Words of Jesus* (New York: Macmillan, 1993), p. 5.

7. Funk et al., p. 16.

8. Funk et al., p. 19.

9. Funk et al., p. 2.

10. Funk et al., pp. 5, 35.

11. Craig Blomberg, "The Seventy-Four 'Scholars': Who Does the Jesus Seminar Really Speak For?" in *Christian Research Journal,* Fall 1994, p. 29.

12. John Wenham, *Redating Matthew, Mark and Luke* (Downers Grove, IL: InterVarsity, 1992), p. 3.

13. Charlotte Allen, "The Search for a No-Frills Jesus," *The Atlantic Monthly,* December 1996, p. 67.

14. Allen, p. 56.

15. Wenham, p. 42.

16. Gregory A. Boyd, *Cynic, Sage or Son of God?* (Wheaton, IL: Bridge Point, 1995), p. 142.

17. Boyd, p. 142.

18. William Lane Craig, *The Son Rises* (Chicago: Moody Press, 1981), pp. 135-136.

19. Michael J. Wilkins and J.P. Moreland, "Introduction: The Furor Surrounding Jesus," in Wilkins and Moreland, *Jesus Under Fire*, pp. 6, 11.

Section Four—Conclusion

1. *Encyclopedia Britannica*, Macropaedia, vol. 2, p. 880.

2. Robert B. Downs, *Books That Changed the World* (New York: New American Library/Mentor, rev., 1983), p. 40.

3. Keith N. Schoville, *Biblical Archaeology in Focus* (Grand Rapids, MI: Baker, 1978), p. 156.

4. Citations taken from Frank S. Meade, *The Encyclopedia of Religious Quotations*; Rhoda Tripp, *The International Thesaurus of Quotations*; Ralph L. Woods, *The World Treasury of Religious Quotations*; Jonathan Green, *Morrow's International Dictionary of Contemporary Quotations*; and http://logosresourcepages.org/quotes .html, compiled by Pastor David L. Brown, PhD, First Baptist Church, Oak Creek, Wisconsin.

ABOUT THE ANKERBERG
THEOLOGICAL RESEARCH INSTITUTE

Asking tough questions...Offering real answers

Mission Statement

The Ankerberg Theological Research Institute (ATRI) is a Christian media organization designed to investigate and answer today's critical questions concerning issues of spirituality, popular culture, and comparative religions.

> *"But in your hearts set apart Christ as Lord. Always be prepared to give an answer to everyone who asks you to give the reason for the hope that you have. But do this with gentleness and respect, keeping a clear conscience, so that those who speak maliciously against your good behavior in Christ may be ashamed of their slander."*

> —1 Peter 3:15-16

ATRI utilizes five strategies to accomplish this mission:

- *The John Ankerberg Show*. Our award-winning weekly TV program is broadcast into all 50 states and 200 countries worldwide via satellite. Our documentaries have also been featured as nationwide television specials.

- *ATRI Radio*. ATRI reaches thousands of people through its weekend one-hour program and one-minute daily radio commentary airing on nearly 700 outlets.

- *JohnAnkerberg.org*. ATRI's Web site reaches over 3.5 million unique visitors per year from 184 countries.

- *ATRI Resources*. In addition to nearly 100 combined published books and 3 million books sold by ATRI authors in 16 languages, ATRI's resources include over 2,500 free online articles, audio, and video programs.

- *ATRI Events.* Founder Dr. John Ankerberg has personally spoken to over 1 million people during his speaking engagements and seminars in dozens of countries spanning five continents.

Due to ATRI's advanced research and long-standing work, founder and president Dr. John Ankerberg is regularly quoted by media including NBC, ABC, Daystar, and INSP. A board member for many Christian media organizations, Dr. Ankerberg also serves on the board of directors for the National Religious Broadcasters Association (NRB).

Expert Resources from Harvest House

TAKING A STAND FOR THE BIBLE
John Ankerberg and Dillon Burroughs

Many so-called experts today are spreading inaccurate or biased information about the Bible. Ankerberg and Burroughs have written *Taking a Stand for the Bible* to help set the record straight. Along the way, they answer the most important questions both Christians and non-Christians are asking, including:

- How did we get the Bible?
- How accurate is the Bible?
- Is the Bible still relevant to us today?

You'll find helpful and well-documented answers backed by careful research and exclusive interviews with some of today's top theology and Bible history scholars, including Dr. Craig Blomberg, Dr. Darrell Bock, Dr. Gary Habermas, and Dr. N.T. Wright. Together they point to remarkable evidence that affirms the Bible's integrity and reliability.

COMMONLY MISUNDERSTOOD BIBLE VERSES
Clear Explanations for the Difficult Passages

Ron Rhodes

Popular Bible teacher Ron Rhodes has appeared on many TV and radio shows and spoken at countless churches, conferences, rallies, and seminars. At most of these events, people have asked him to explain difficult Bible verses. Now you can learn from his concise and easy-to-understand responses to commonly asked questions like these:

"The LORD said to Satan...he is in your hands" (Job 2:6).

How could a loving God allow Job, an upright man, to suffer?

"Ask and it will be given to you" (Matthew 7:7).

Despite Jesus' promise, some prayers don't get answered. Why not?

"Anyone who has faith in me...will do even greater things" (John 14:12).

Can Christians perform greater miracles than Jesus did?

Ron's responses to frequently misunderstood Bible verses will stimulate your personal growth and bolster your confidence in the Word of God.

HANDBOOK OF BIBLICAL EVIDENCES

The Facts On Jesus • Creation • The Bible

John Ankerberg and John Weldon

"Always be ready to give an answer to everyone who asks you to give the reason for the hope that you have."—1 Peter 3:15

- "Hasn't evolution proved that Genesis is wrong?"
- "Isn't the Bible filled with historical and scientific errors?"
- "What compelling evidence is there that Jesus rose from the dead?"

If you were challenged like that, how would you respond? In *Handbook of Biblical Evidences*, you'll find the answers to these and other tough questions, backed up by in-depth research and solid analysis.

Our world is filled with people asking such questions about God, the meaning of life, and the truth of the Bible. If you've been hesitant to talk about your faith for fear of not knowing what to say, now you can be prepared to explain your faith to those looking for answers.

To read a sample chapter of these or other Harvest House books, go to www.harvesthousepublishers.com

SEARCHING FOR THE ORIGINAL BIBLE

Who Wrote It and Why? • Is It Reliable? • Has the Text Changed over Time?

Randall Price

> *"A fine book for lay and professional readers alike."*
>
> PUBLISHERS WEEKLY MAGAZINE

Lost...destroyed...hidden...forgotten. For many centuries, no one has seen any of the original biblical documents.

How can you know whether today's Bible is true to them?

The Bible claims to be a communication from God—a text that is completely reliable. Can you still be confident of this? What about allegations by scholars and in the media that the "Lost Gospels" prove the early church changed the Scripture? Noted researcher and archaeologist Randall Price brings his expert knowledge to tackle crucial questions:

- What happened to the original Bible text? If we don't have it, what do we have?

- How was the text handed down to our time? Can you trust that process?

- Should other books be included in our Bible—like the "Lost Gospels"?

- How can the text of the original documents be recovered today?

- What about the Bible's claim to be inspired and inerrant?

Current evidence upholds the historic views of orthodox Christianity more strongly than ever. Today's Bible remains the authoritative record of God's revelation for every person—a Book you can build your life and faith on.

> *"Graphically and accurately traces the...important work that lies behind obtaining the authentic words that our Lord revealed to his prophets and apostles in the Scriptures."*
>
> WALTER C. KAISER JR.
> President Emeritus, Gordon-Conwell Theological Seminary